Scripture Songs

of
Love, Joy, and Peace

Familiar words from the inspired Word of God
- memorable music
- chords for keyboard and guitar
- arranged in alphabetical order

May the music speak to your heart;
May the words feed your soul.

Words from the King James version.
Music composed and arranged by Gary Hullquist, MD

King Solomon "spake three thousand proverbs,
and his songs were a thousand and five."
1Kings 4:32

"God my maker, Who giveth songs in the night"
Job 35:10

World rights reserved. This book or any portion thereof may not be copied or reproduced in any form or manner whatever, except as provided by law, without the written permission of the publisher, except by a reviewer who may quote brief passages in a review.

The author assumes full responsibility for the accuracy of all facts and quotations as cited in this book. The opinions expressed in this book are the author's personal views and interpretations, and do not necessarily reflect those of the publisher.

This book is provided with the understanding that the publisher is not engaged in giving spiritual, legal, medical, or other professional advice. If authoritative advice is needed, the reader should seek the counsel of a competent professional.

―――――――――――

Copyright © 2020 C. Gary Hullquist, MD
Copyright © 2020 TEACH Services, Inc.
ISBN-13: 978-1-4796-1333-5 (Paperback)
ISBN-13: 978-1-4796-1334-2 (ePub)

Library of Congress Control Number: 2020915031

Talking Rock Sabbath Chapel
1250 W. Price Creek Rd
PO Box 39
Talking Rock, GA 30175
706-406-1945

Mp3 vocal and accompaniment tracks at
www.trsc.today/php/Songs.php

August 2020

TEACH Services, Inc.
PUBLISHING
www.TEACHServices.com • (800) 367-1844

All Power is Given Him
Matthew 28:18-20

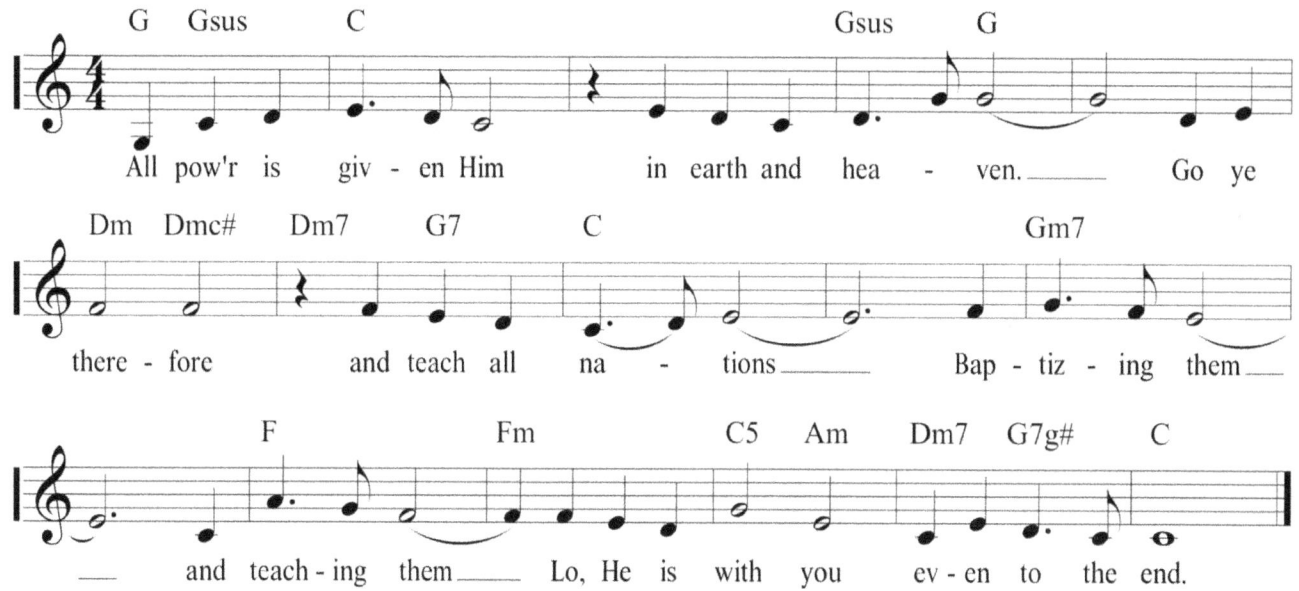

The Father loveth the Son and hath given all things into His hands. John 3:35. Wherefore God also hath highly exalted Him, and given Him a name which is above every name. Philippians 2:9. Being made so much better than the angels, as He hath by inheritance obtained a more excellent name than they. Hebrews 1:4. God…hath in these last days spoken unto us by His Son, whom He hath appointed heir of all things, by whom also He made the worlds. Hebrews 1:1,2. Christ, the power of God, and the wisdom of God. 1Corinthians 1:24.

And It Shall Come To Pass
Isaiah 66:22,23

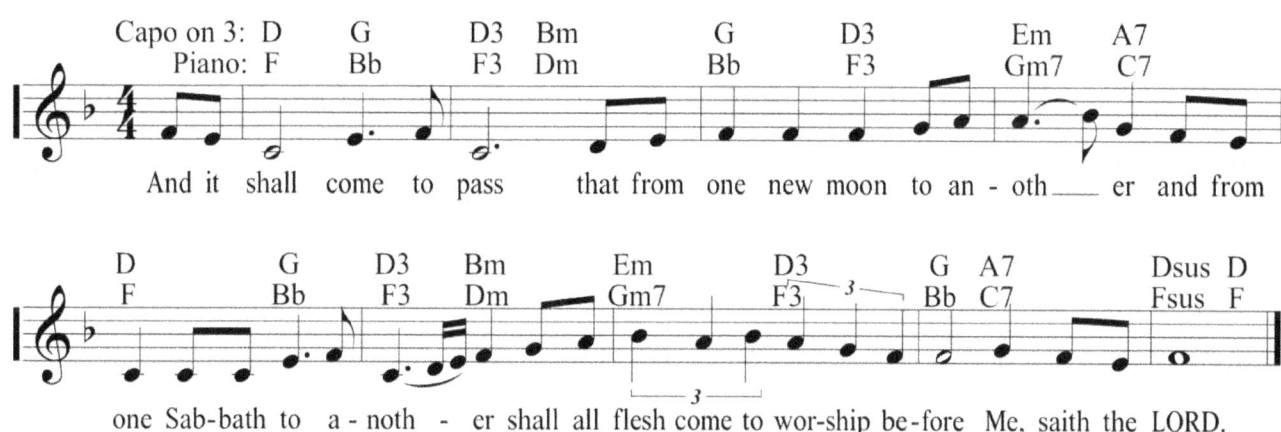

3 And the Glory
John 17:22,23

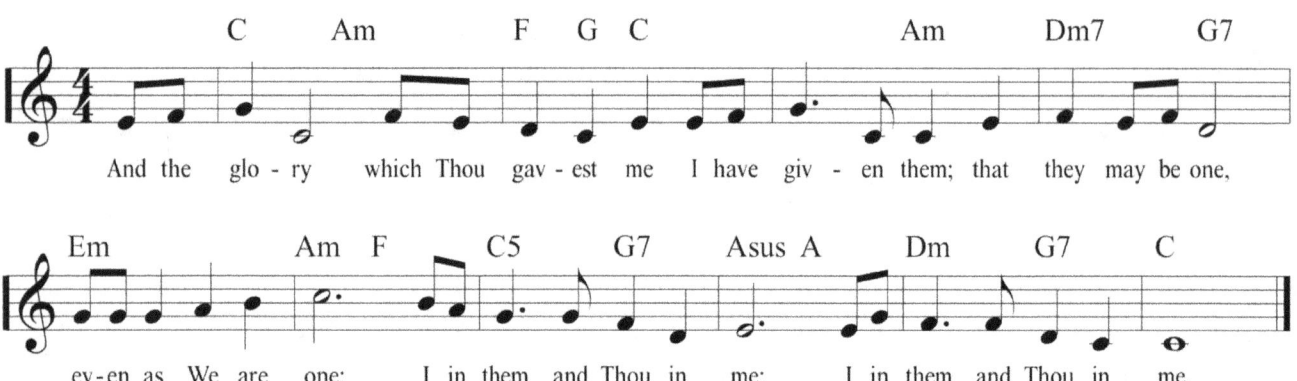

And the glory which Thou gavest me I have given them; that they may be one, even as We are one: I in them and Thou in me; I in them and Thou in me.

4 And This is Life
John 17:3; 2John 3; 1Corinthians 8:6

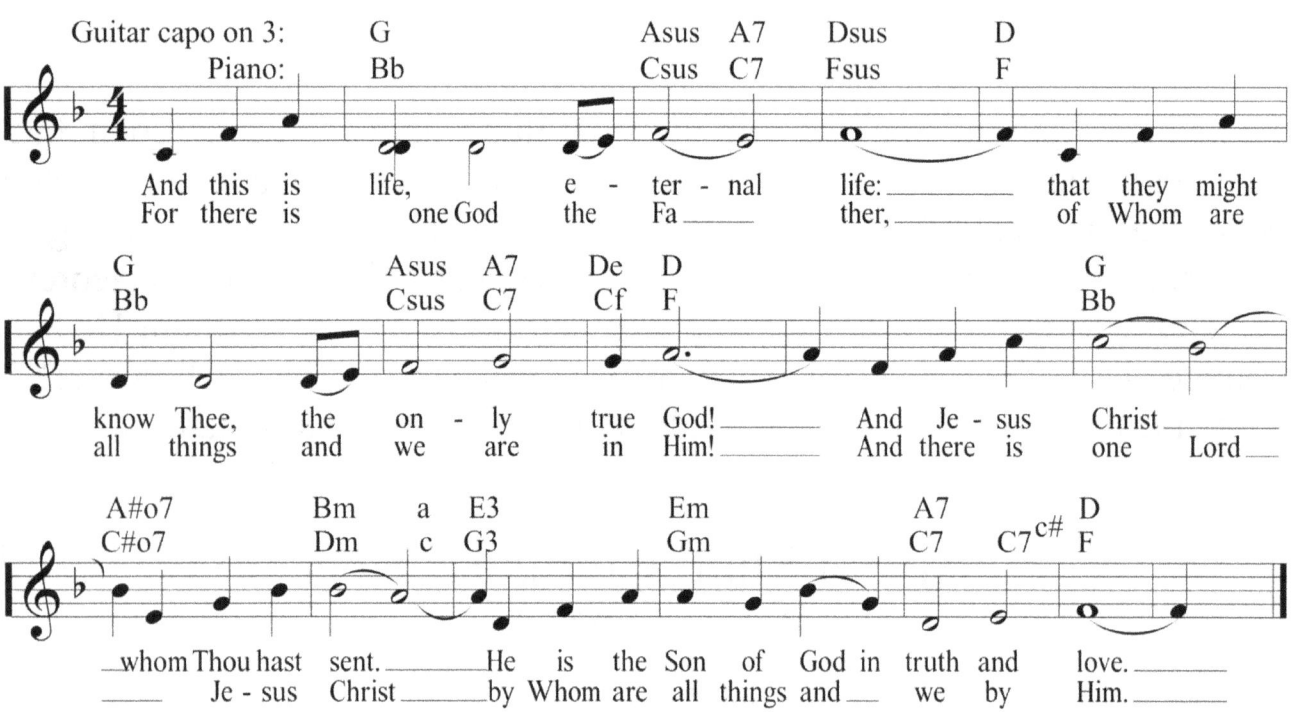

And this is life, eternal life: that they might know Thee, the only true God! And Jesus Christ whom Thou hast sent. He is the Son of God in truth and love.

For there is one God the Father, of Whom are all things and we are in Him! And there is one Lord Jesus Christ by Whom are all things and we by Him.

Ye turned to God from idols to serve the true and living God; and to wait for His Son from heaven, whom He raised from the dead, even Jesus. 1Thessalonians 1:9,10. For there is one God, and one mediator between God and men, the man Christ Jesus. 1Timothy 2:5. Blessed be the God and Father of our Lord Jesus Christ, Ephesians 1:3; 1Peter 1:3, the God and Father of our Lord Jesus Christ. 2Corinthians 11:31.

Angel of His Presence
Isaiah 63:9,10

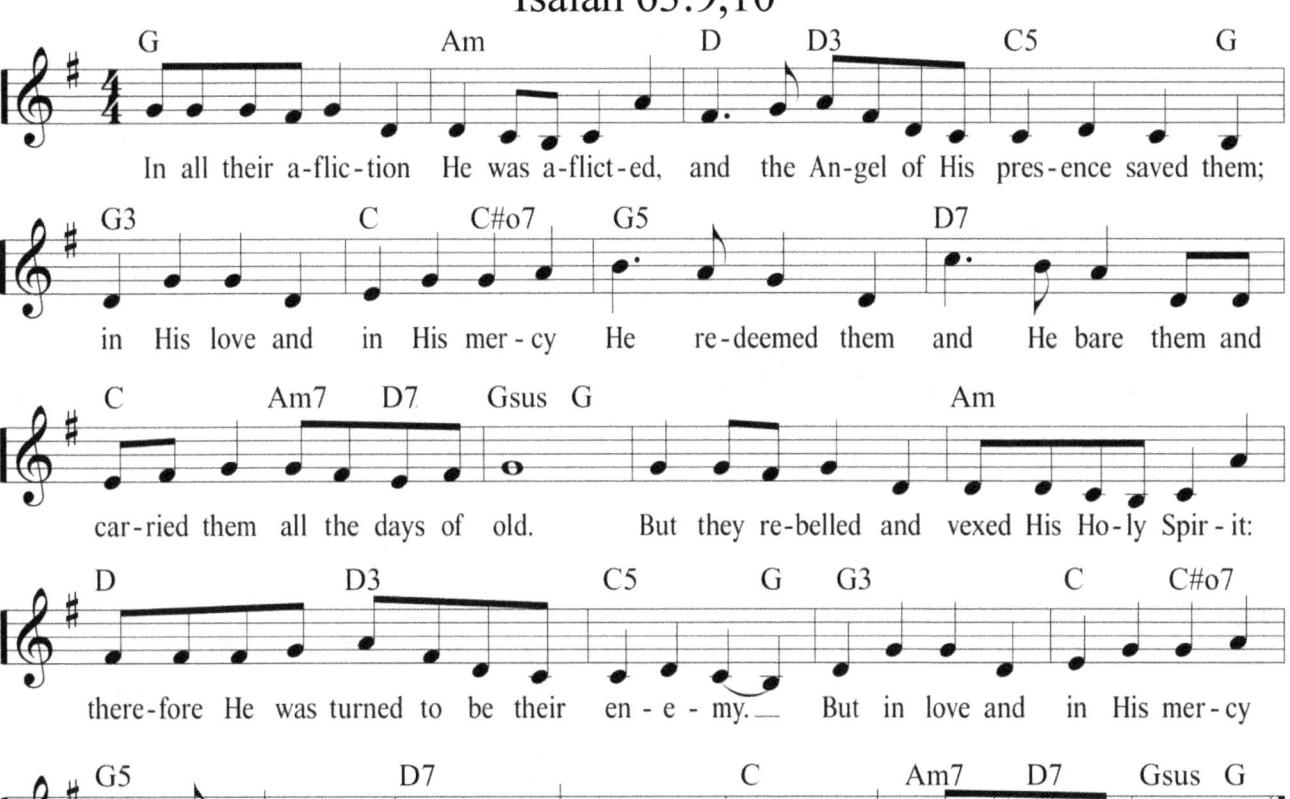

Angel of the Lord
Psalm 34:7,8

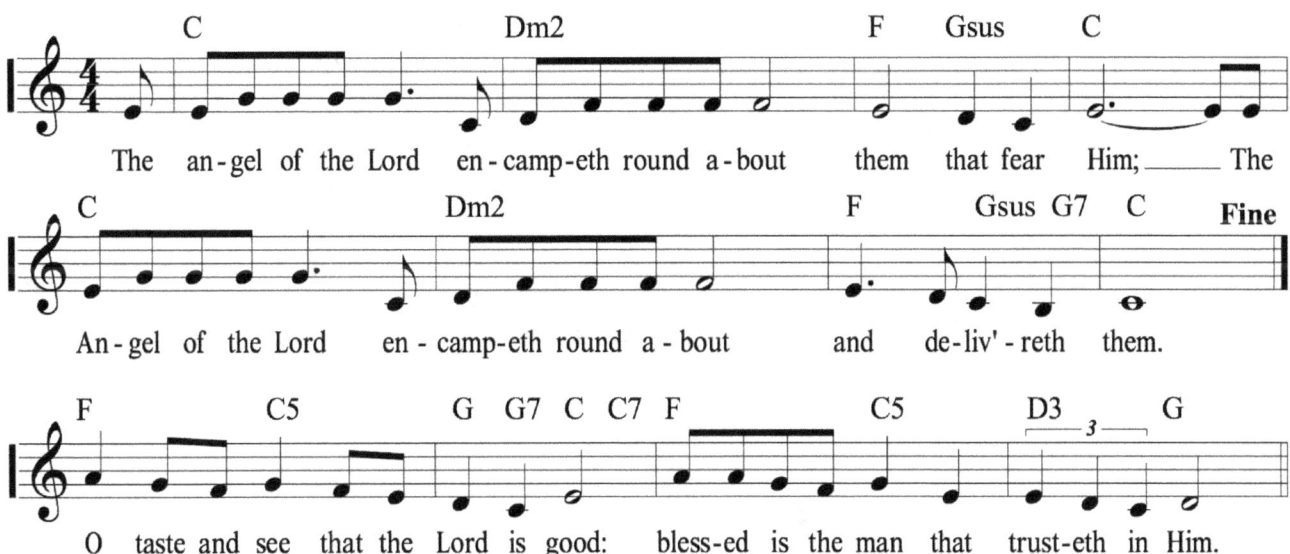

7 Arise Shine
Isaiah 60:1; Revelation 18:1

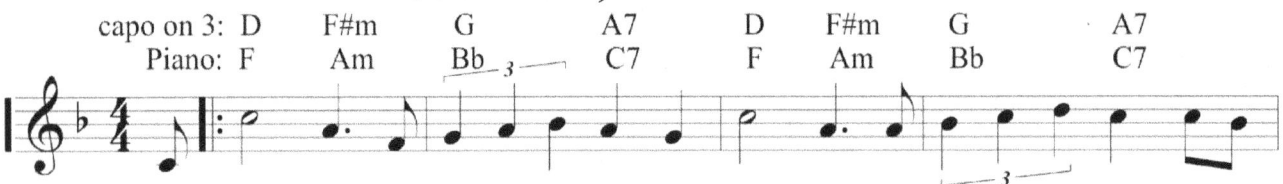
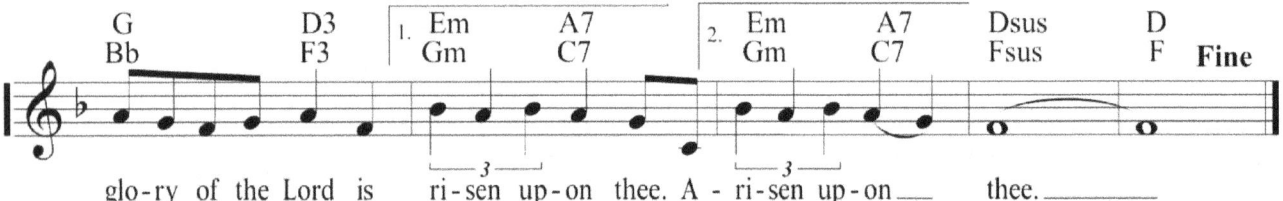

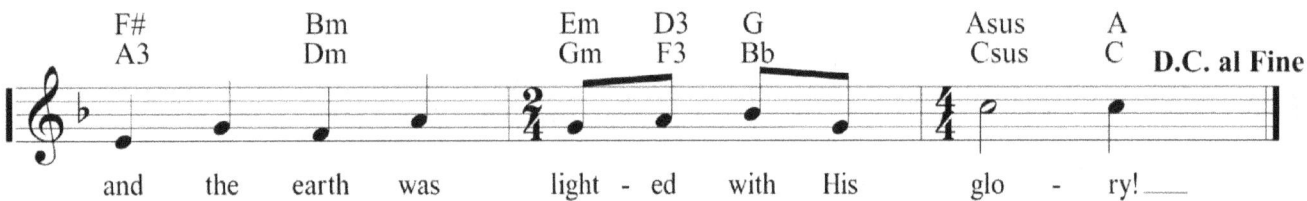

8 As Eagles
Isaiah 40:31

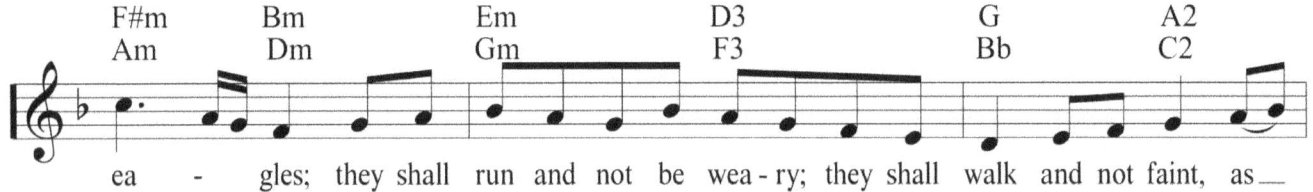
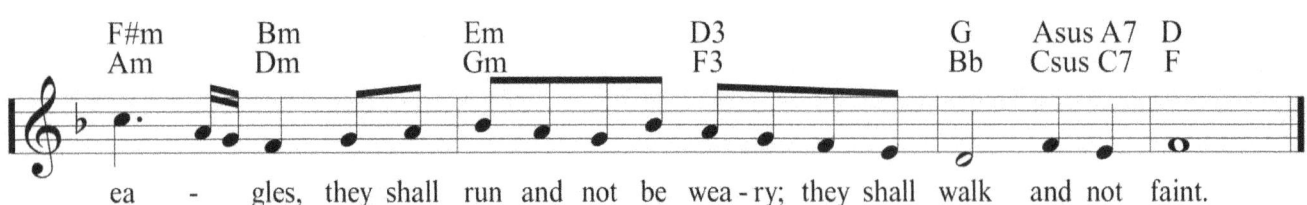

As Christ Was Raised Up
Romans 6:4

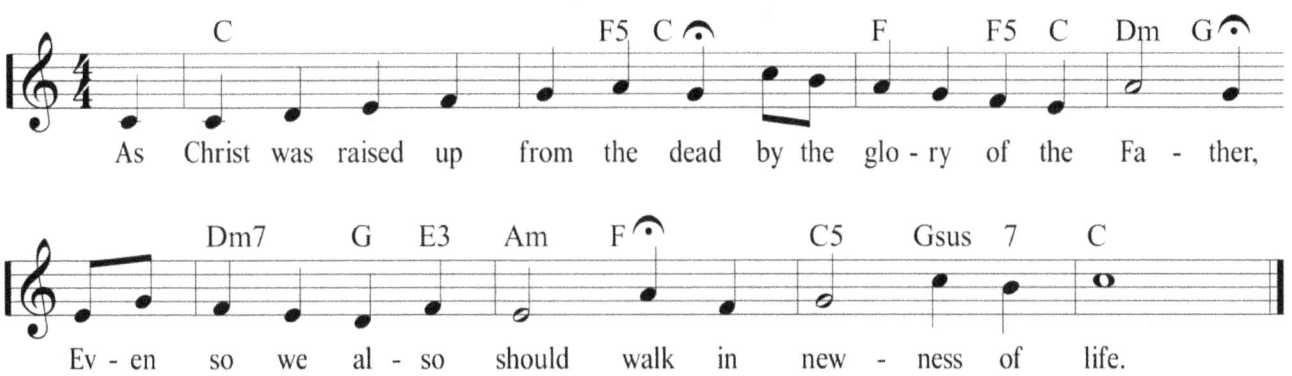

As the Father Hath Life in Himself
John 5:25, 26

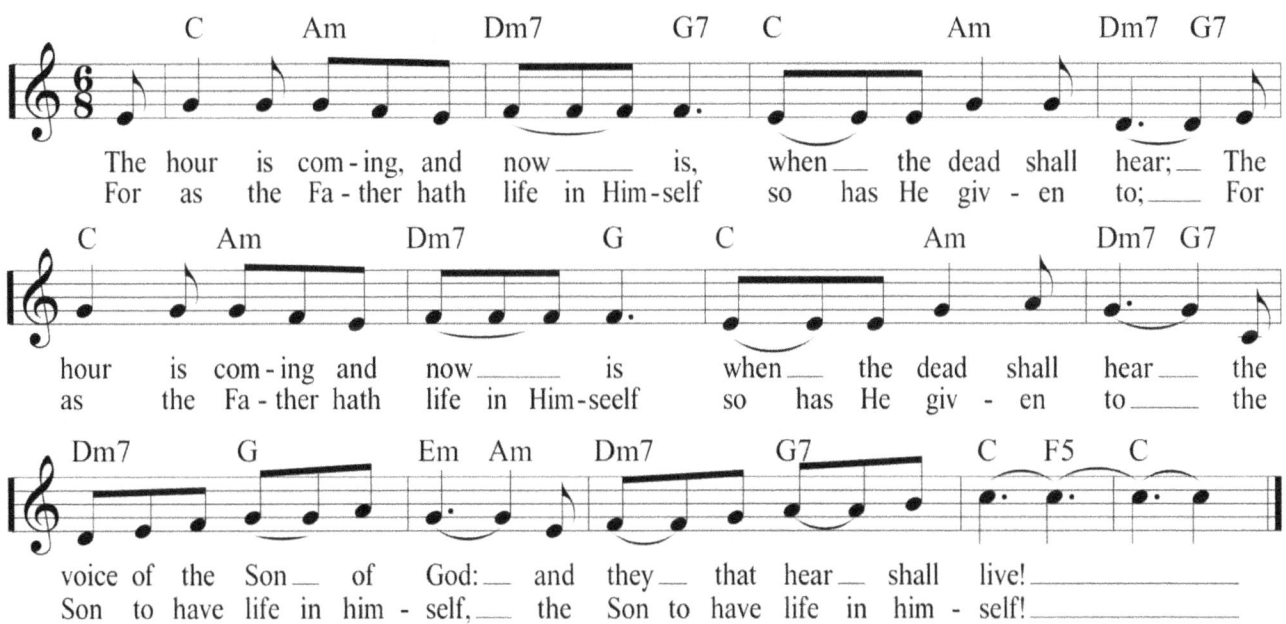

God hath given to us eternal life, and this life is in His Son. 1John 5:11. For the Lord Himself shall descend from heaven with a shout, with the voice of the archangel, and with the trump of God: and the dead in Christ shall rise first. 1Thessalonians 4:16. All things are delivered unto me of my Father. Matthew 11:27. I am come that they might have life. John 10:10.

11 As the Mountains

Psalm 125:2

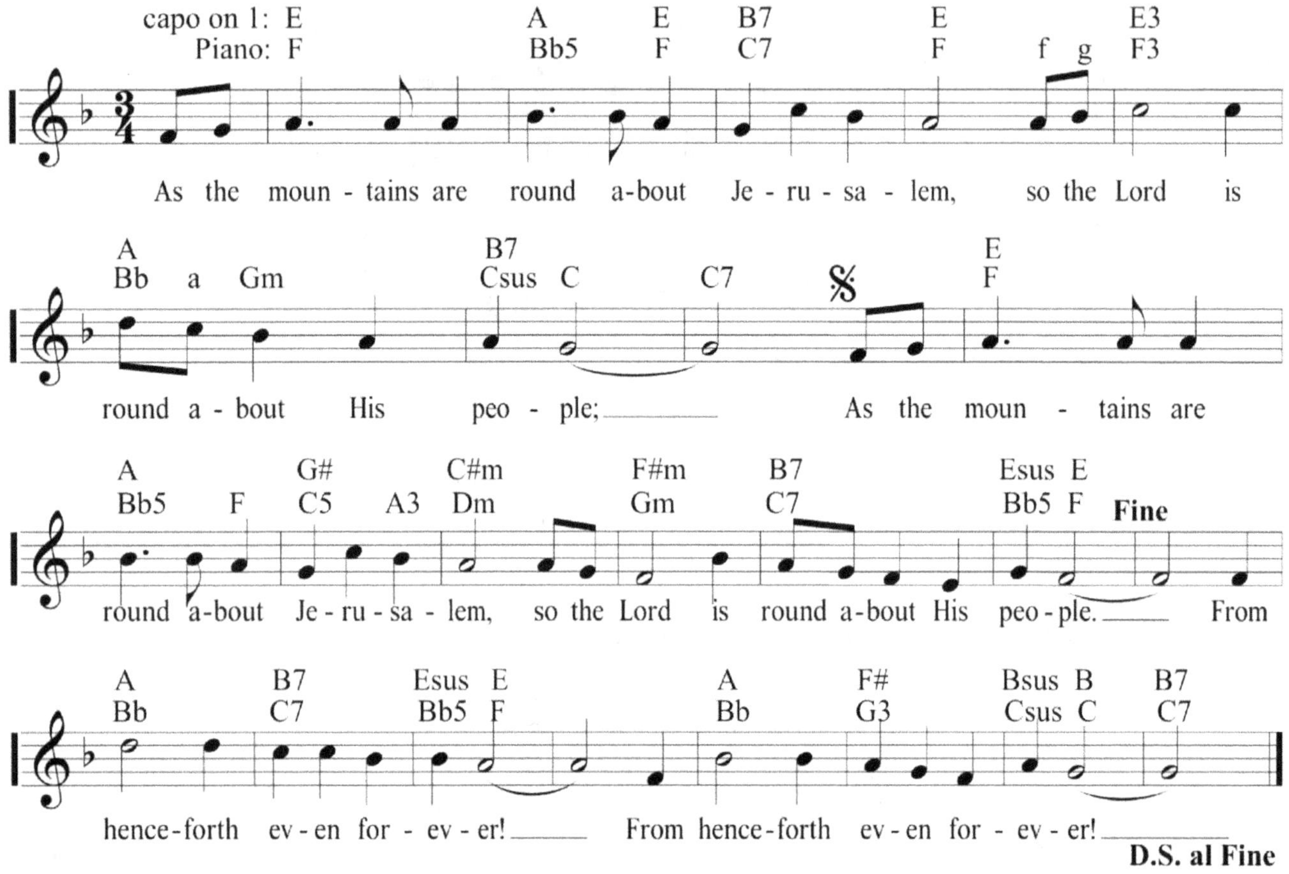
capo on 1: E A E B7 E E3
Piano: F Bb5 F C7 F f g F3
As the moun - tains are round a-bout Je - ru - sa - lem, so the Lord is
A B7 E
Bb a Gm Csus C C7 F
round a - bout His peo - ple; As the moun - tains are
A G# C#m F#m B7 Esus E
Bb5 F C5 A3 Dm Gm C7 Bb5 F
Fine
round a-bout Je - ru - sa - lem, so the Lord is round a-bout His peo - ple. From
A B7 Esus E A F# Bsus B B7
Bb C7 Bb5 F Bb G3 Csus C C7
hence-forth ev - en for - ev - er! From hence-forth ev - en for - ev - er!
D.S. al Fine

12 Be Careful for Nothing

Philippians 4:6

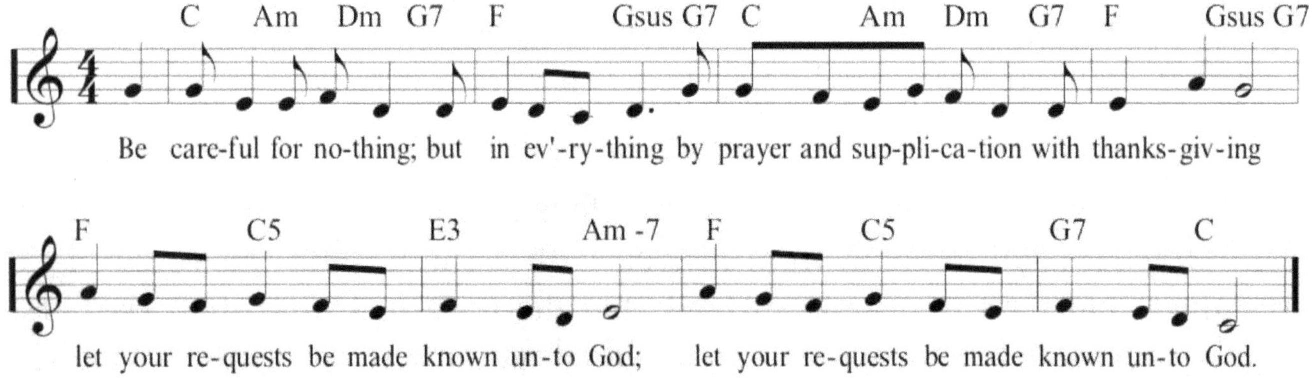
C Am Dm G7 F Gsus G7 C Am Dm G7 F Gsus G7
Be care-ful for no-thing; but in ev'-ry-thing by prayer and sup-pli-ca-tion with thanks-giv-ing
F C5 E3 Am -7 F C5 G7 C
let your re-quests be made known un-to God; let your re-quests be made known un-to God.

Be Glad Then
Joel 2:23

13

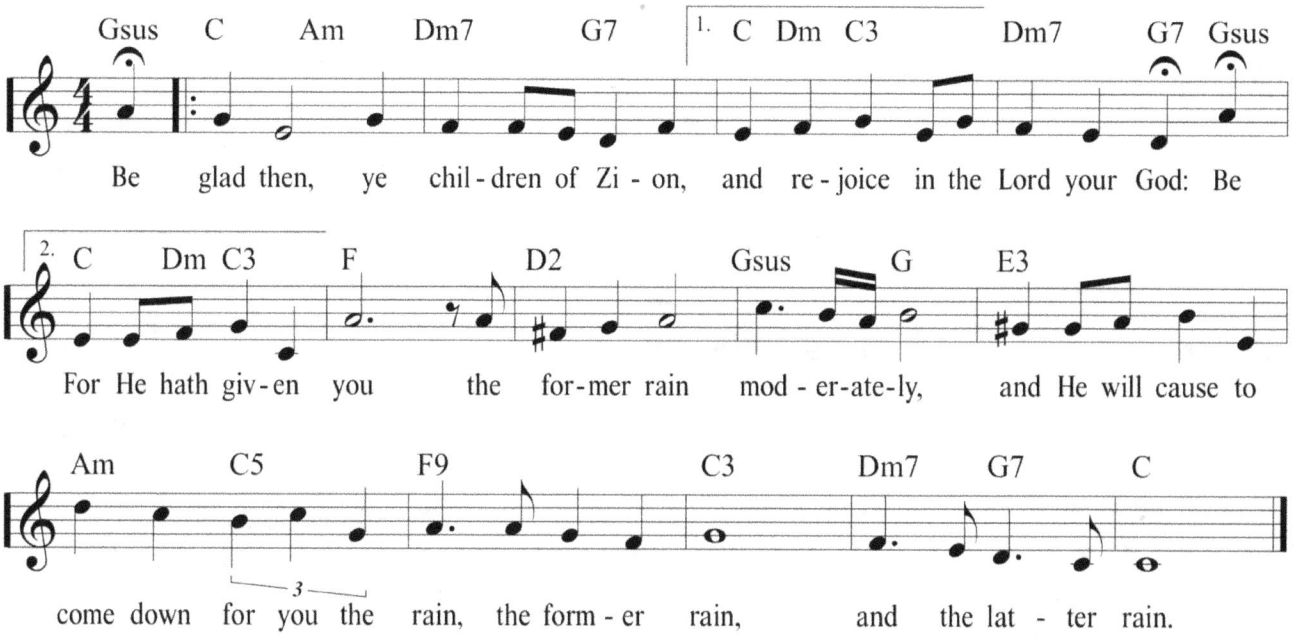

Be glad then, ye chil-dren of Zi-on, and re-joice in the Lord your God: Be
For He hath giv-en you the for-mer rain mod-er-ate-ly, and He will cause to
come down for you the rain, the form-er rain, and the lat-ter rain.

Then shall we know if we follow on to know the LORD: His going forth is prepared as the morning; and He shall come unto us as the rain, as the latter and former rain upon the earth. Hosea 6:3. That your sins may be blotted out, when the times of refreshing shall come from the presence of the Lord. And He shall send Jesus Christ. Acts 3:19,20. He shall come down like rain upon the mown grass: as showers that water the earth. Psalm 72:6.

Be Strong
Deuteronomy 31:6

14

Be strong and of a good cour-age, fear not, nor be a-fraid of them: for the
Lord thy God, He doth go with thee. He will not fail thee, nor for-sake thee.

15 Before the Foundation of the World
Ephesians 1:3,4,6,7

Behold the Bridegroom Cometh
Matthew 25:5,6,10

The kingdom of heaven is like unto a certain King, which made a marriage for His Son, and sent forth His servants to call them that were bidden to the wedding. Matthew 22:2,3. Let us be glad and rejoice, and give honour to Him: for the marriage of the Lamb is come, and His wife hath made herself ready… Blessed are they which are called unto the marriage supper of the Lamb. Revelation 19:7,9.

17 Behold the Fowls of the Air
Matthew 6:26,28,29

Therefore take no thought, saying, What shall we eat? or, What shall we drink? Or, Wherewithal shall we be clothed? For your heavenly Father knoweth that ye have need of all these things. Matthew 6:31,32. If ye then, being evil, know how to give good gifts unto your children, how much more shall your Father which is in heaven give good things to them that ask Him? Matthew 7:11. Your Father which is in heaven…maketh His sun to rise on the evil and on the good, and sendeth rain on the just and on the unjust. Matthew 5:45. It is not the will of my Father which is in heaven, that one of these little ones should perish. Matthew 18:14.

Behold the Lord Passed By 18

1Kings 19:11,12

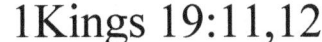

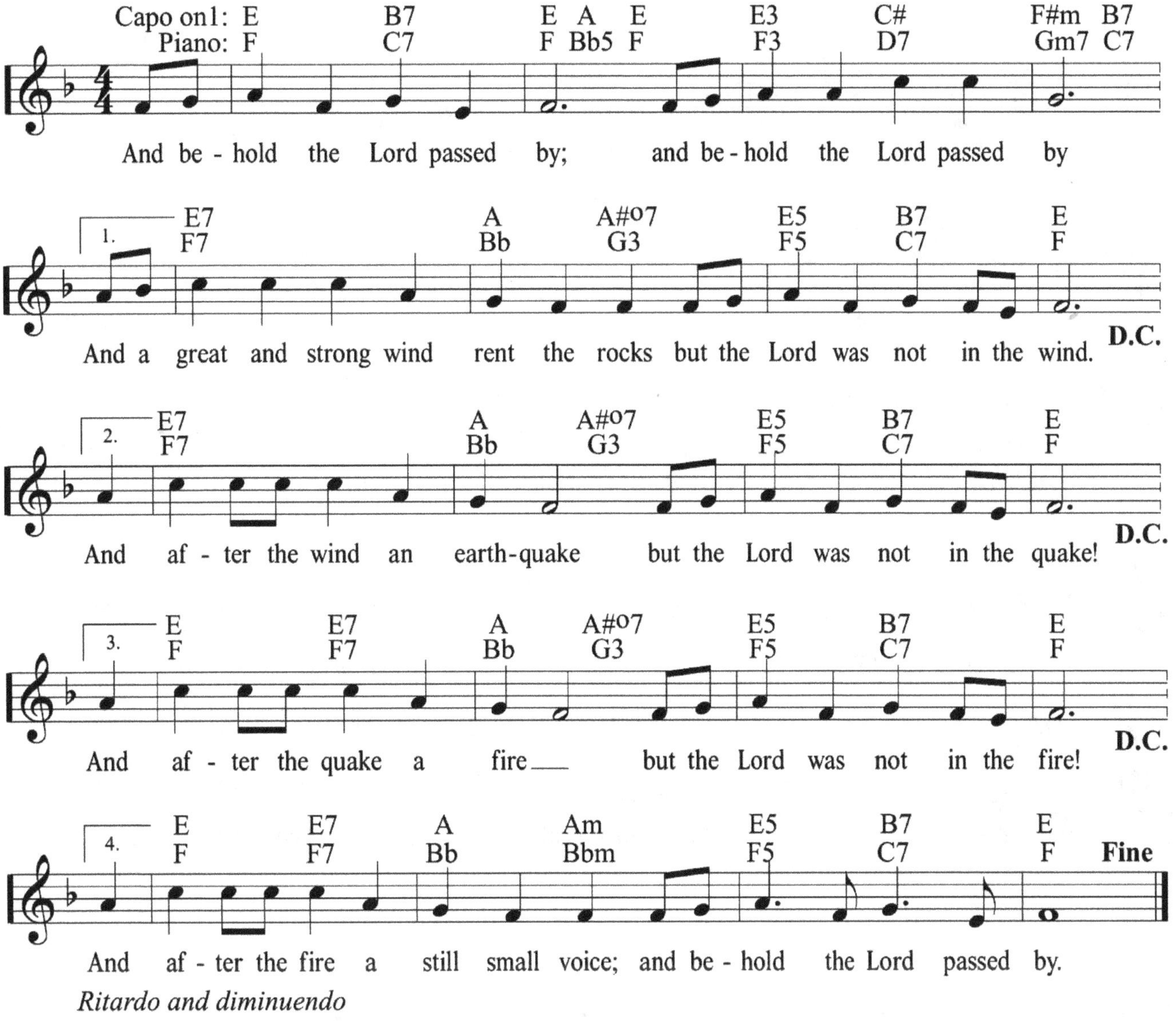
Capo on1: E B7 E A E E3 C# F#m B7
Piano: F C7 F Bb5 F F3 D7 Gm7 C7
And be - hold the Lord passed by; and be - hold the Lord passed by
1. E7 A A#o7 E5 B7 E
F7 Bb G3 F5 C7 F
And a great and strong wind rent the rocks but the Lord was not in the wind. D.C.
2. E7 A A#o7 E5 B7 E
F7 Bb G3 F5 C7 F
And af - ter the wind an earth-quake but the Lord was not in the quake! D.C.
3. E E7 A A#o7 E5 B7 E
F F7 Bb G3 F5 C7 F
And af - ter the quake a fire__ but the Lord was not in the fire! D.C.
4. E E7 A Am E5 B7 E
F F7 Bb Bbm F5 C7 F Fine
And af - ter the fire a still small voice; and be - hold the Lord passed by.
Ritardo and diminuendo

Behold my servant, whom I uphold; mine elect, in whom my soul delighteth …He shall not cry, nor lift up, nor cause His voice to be heard in the street. A bruised reed shall He not break, and the smoking flax shall He not quench. Isaiah 42:1-3. Christ also suffered for us, leaving us an example, that we should follow His steps; who did no sin, neither was guile found in his mouth: who, when He was reviled reviled not again; when He suffered, He threatened not. 1Peter 2:21-23. For the Son of man is not come to destroy men's lives, but to save them. Luke 9:56.

19 Behold the Man Whose Name is the Branch

Zechariah 6:12,13

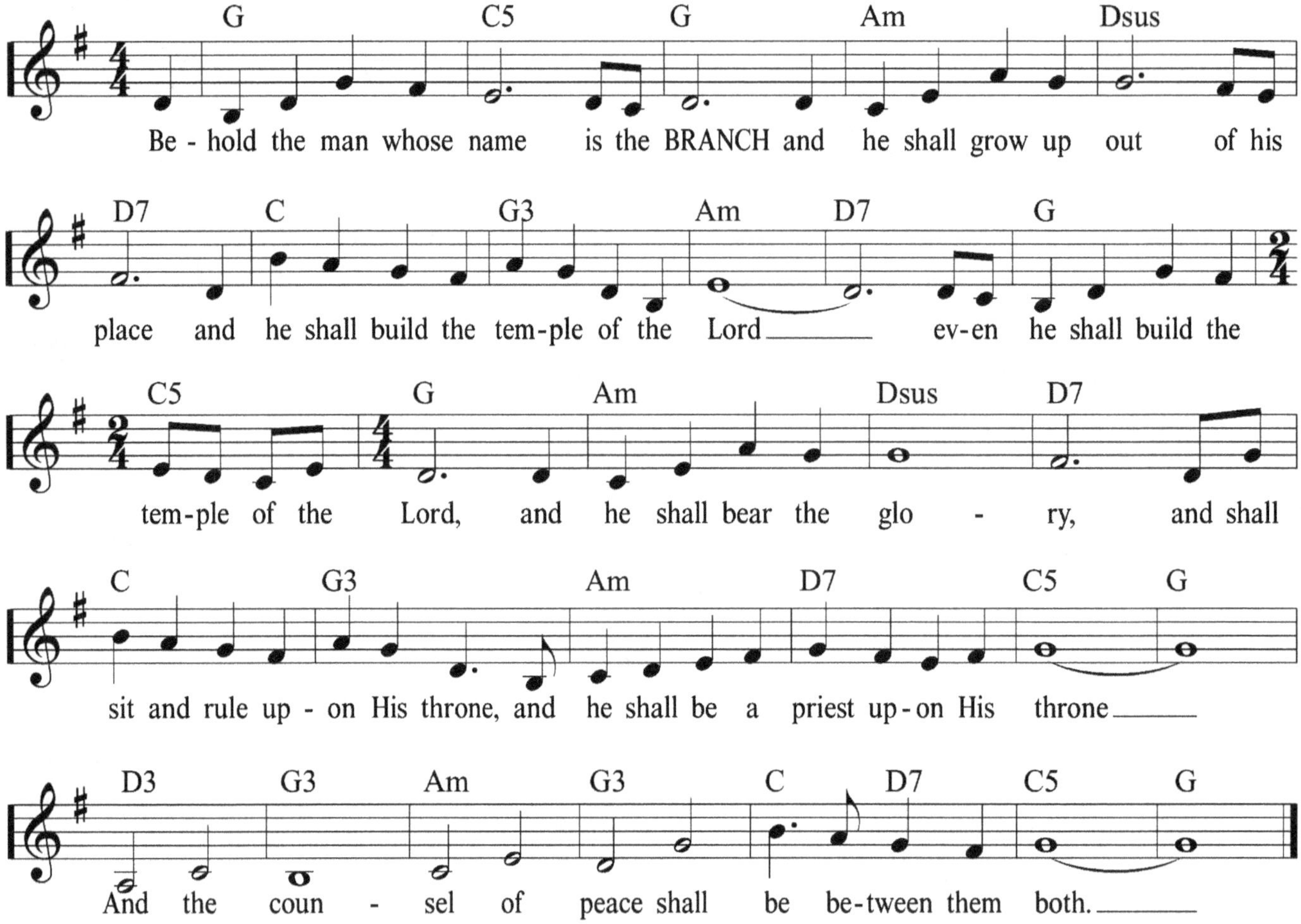
G C5 G Am Dsus
Be - hold the man whose name is the BRANCH and he shall grow up out of his
D7 C G3 Am D7 G
place and he shall build the tem-ple of the Lord ev-en he shall build the
C5 G Am Dsus D7
tem-ple of the Lord, and he shall bear the glo - ry, and shall
C G3 Am D7 C5 G
sit and rule up - on His throne, and he shall be a priest up-on His throne
D3 G3 Am G3 C D7 C5 G
And the coun - sel of peace shall be be-tween them both.

20 Believe in the Lord Your God

2 Chronicles 20:20

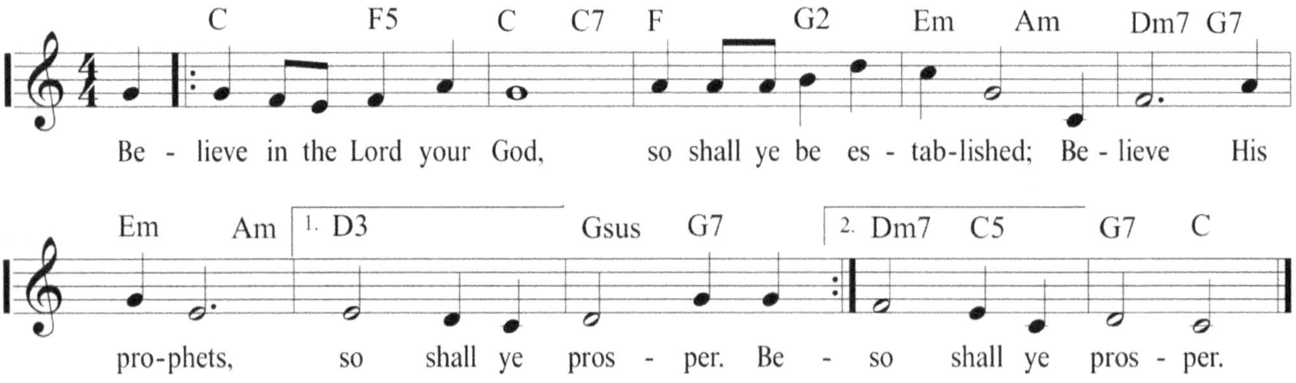
C F5 C C7 F G2 Em Am Dm7 G7
Be - lieve in the Lord your God, so shall ye be es - tab-lished; Be - lieve His
Em Am 1. D3 Gsus G7 2. Dm7 C5 G7 C
pro-phets, so shall ye pros - per. Be - so shall ye pros - per.

Beloved I Wish
3 John 2

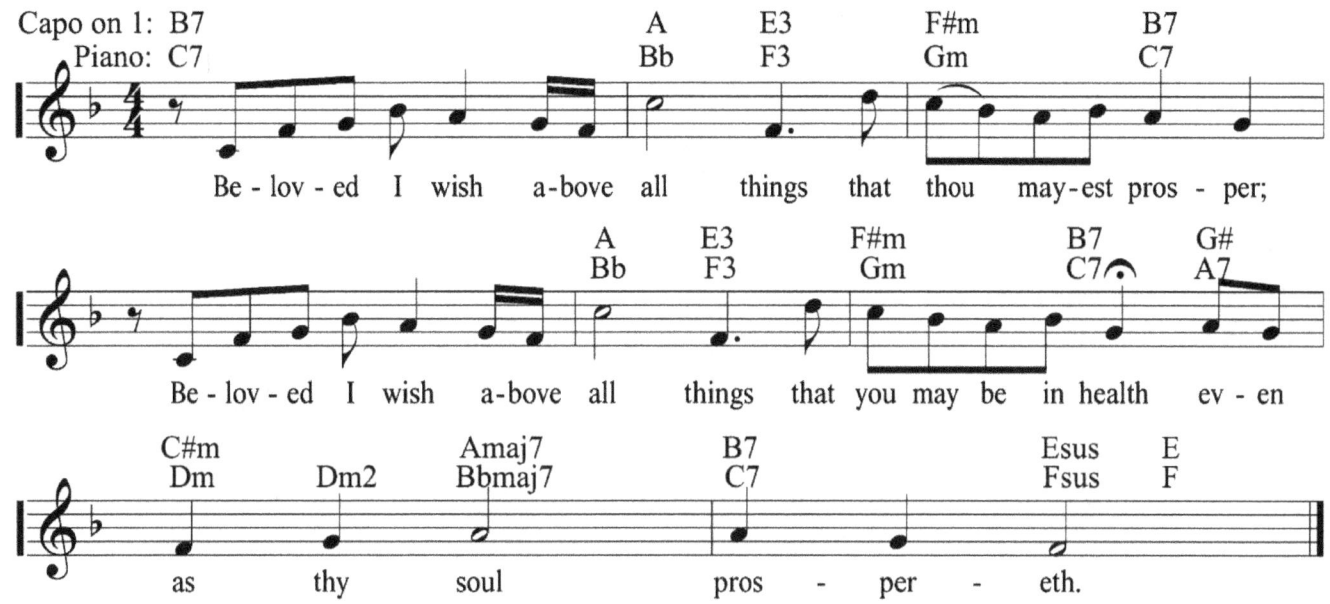

Blessed and Only Potentate
1 Timothy 6:15,16

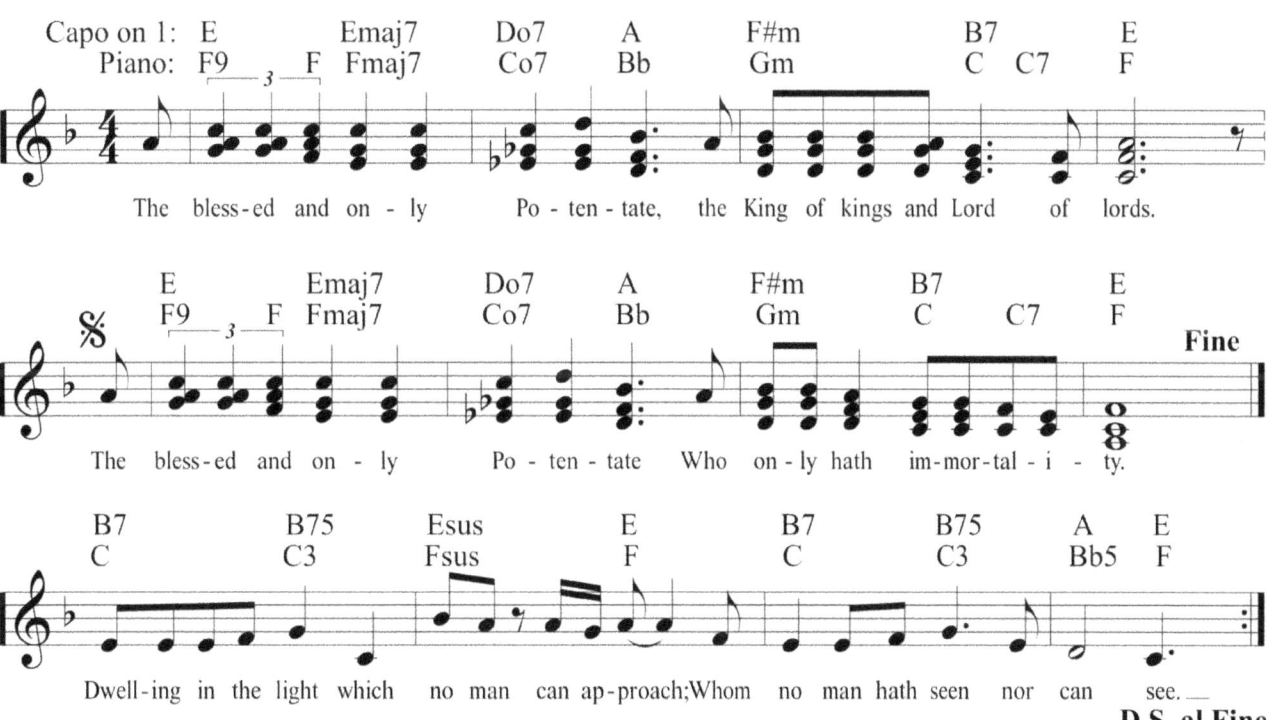

23 Blessed Be God
2 Corinthians 1:3,4

24 Blessed Is Every One
Psalm 128

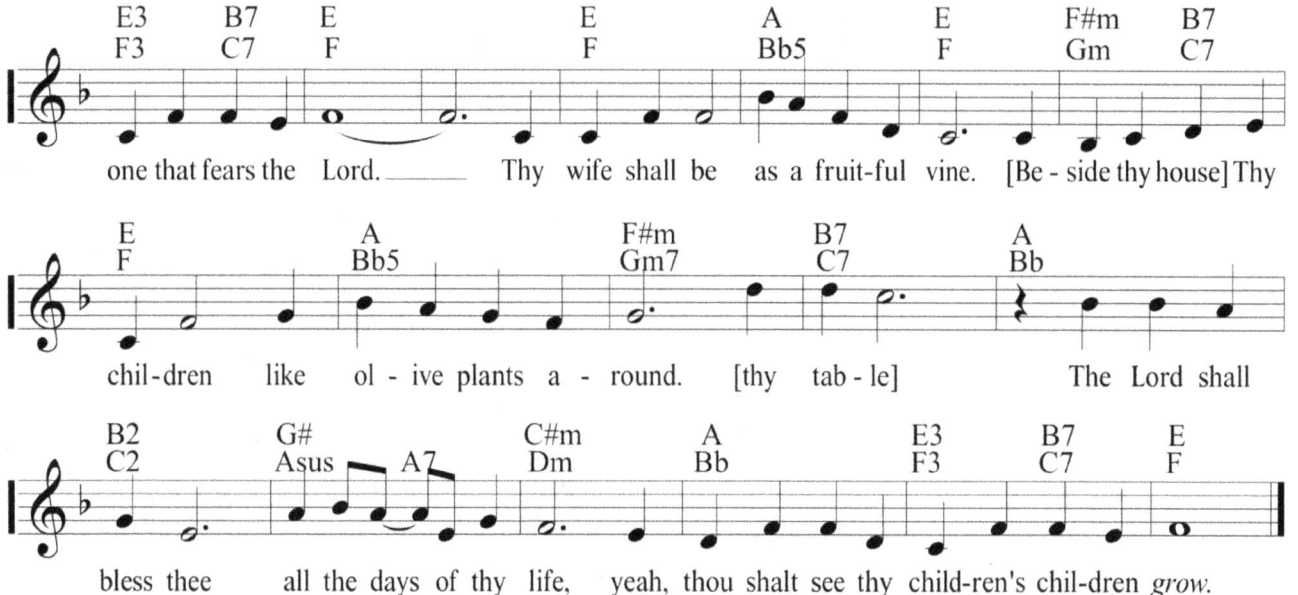

Blessed Is the Man
Psalm 1:1-3

25

26 Boldness to Enter
Hebrews 10:19,20

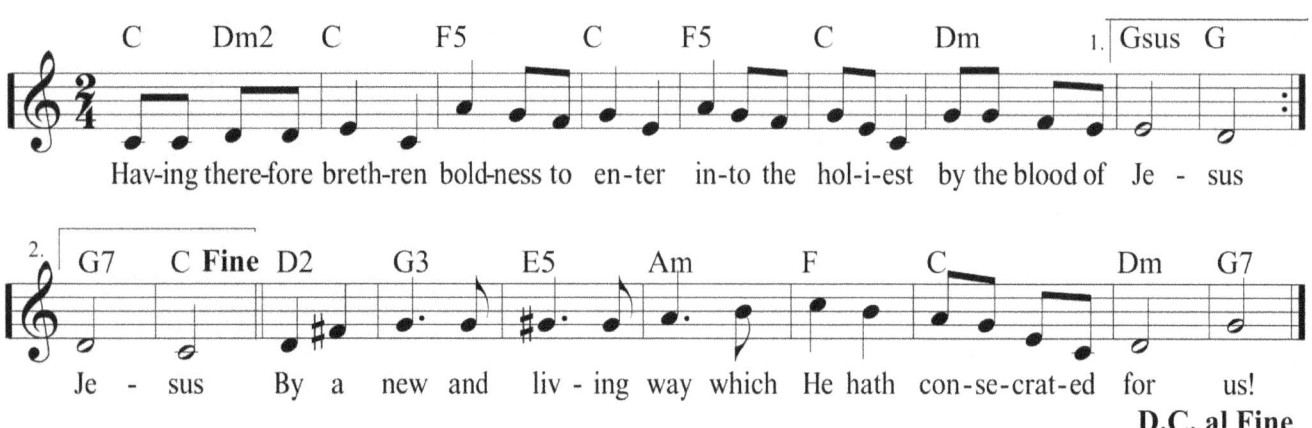

27 By the Word of the Lord
Psalm 33:6,9

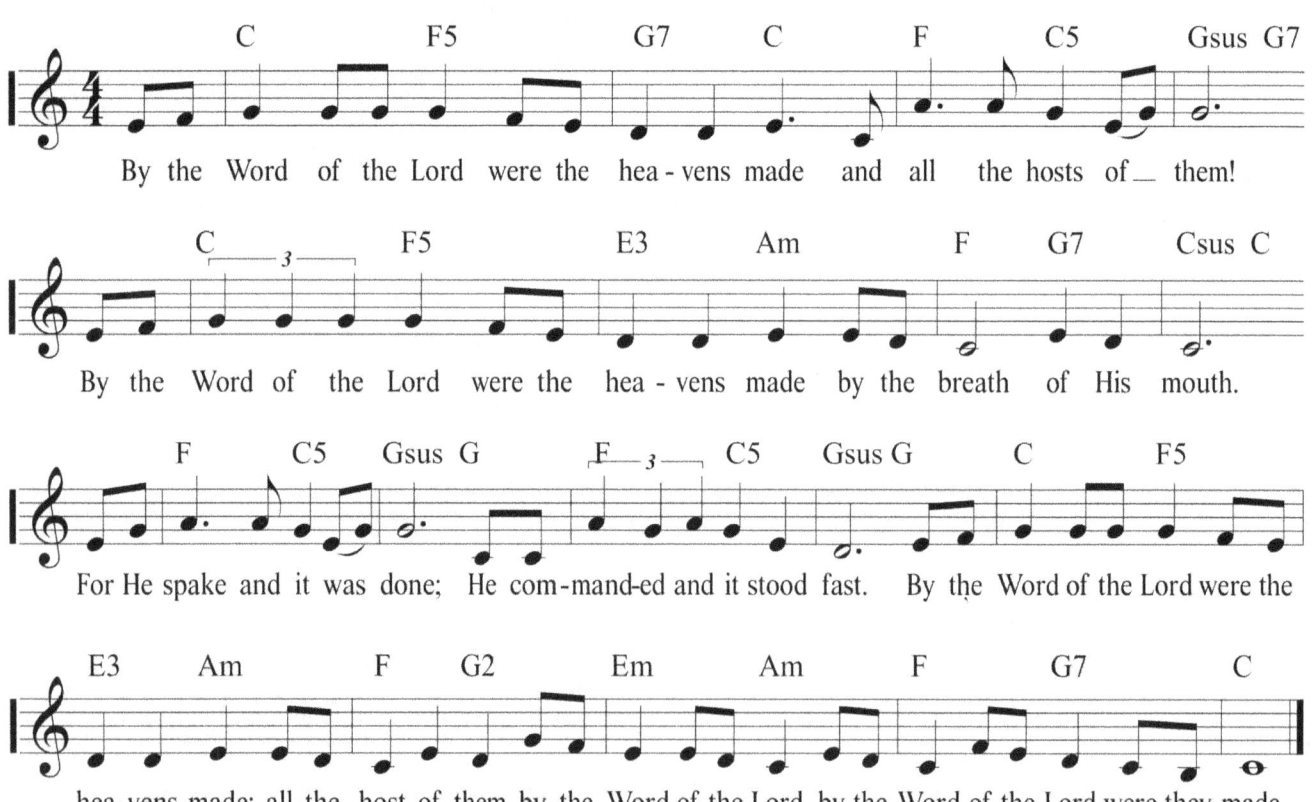

Through faith we understand that the worlds were framed by the word of God, so that things which are seen were not made of things which do appear. Hebrews 11:3. And the Word was made flesh and dwelt among us. John 1:14.

Call Upon Him
Jeremiah 33:3

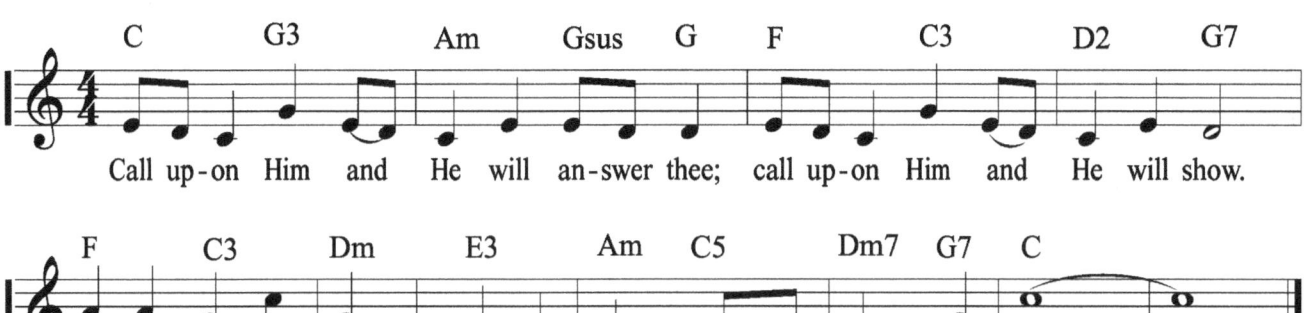

Call Upon the Name of the Lord

Psalm 116:13,17; Isaiah 55:6; 1Kings 18:24; Joshua 24:15;
Psalm 20:7,9,5; Isaiah 40:9; Psalm 102:21,27;113:2,1; Matthew 7:7

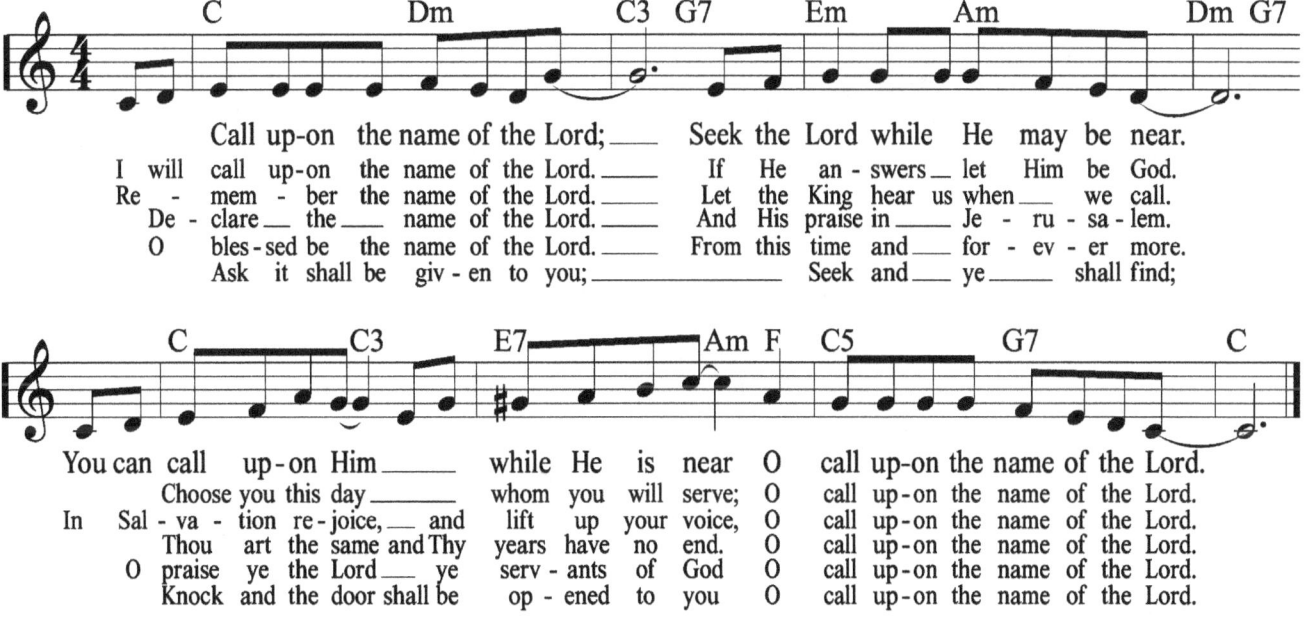

30 Can a Woman Forget?

Isaiah 49:15,16

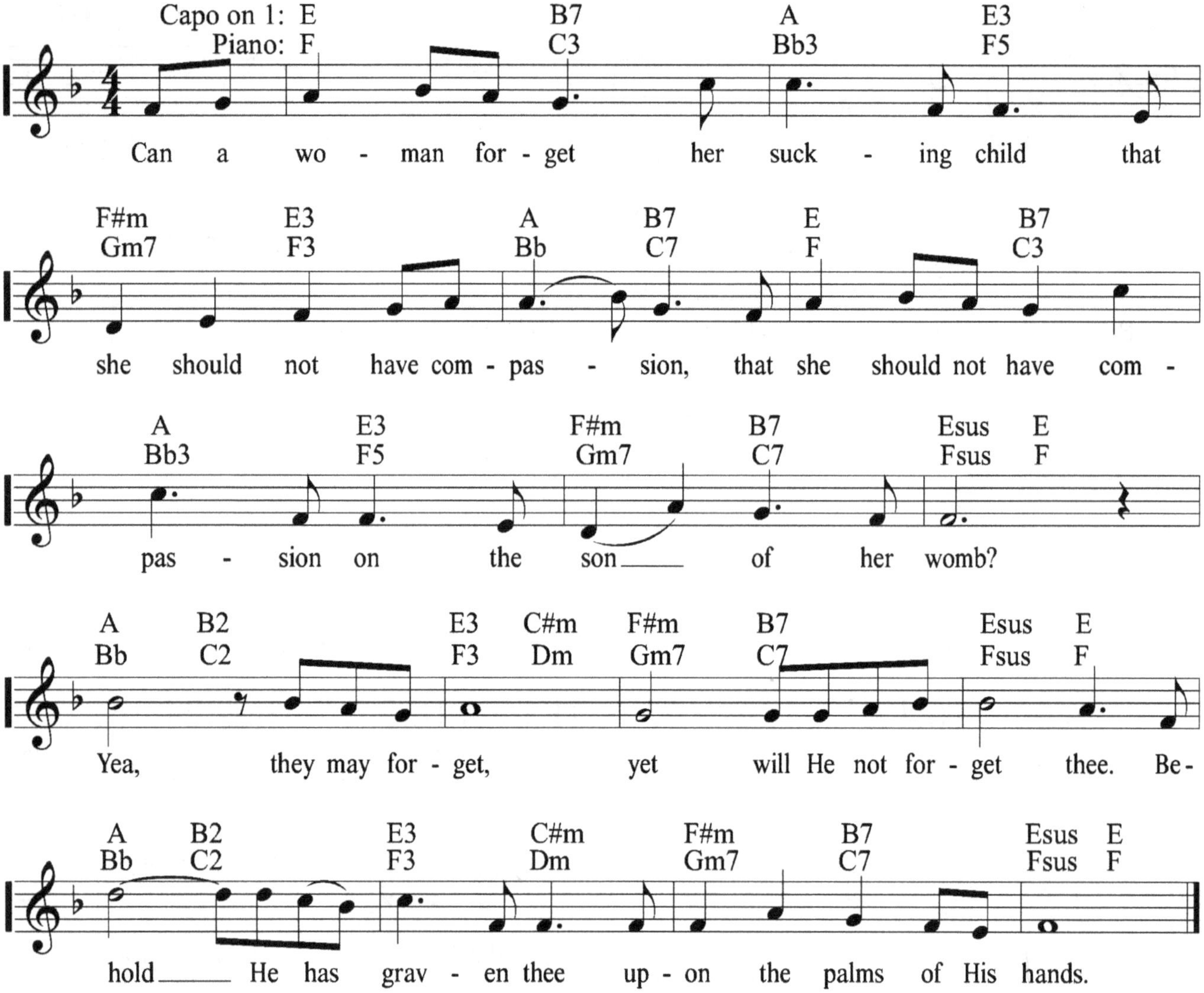
Capo on 1: E B7 A E3
Piano: F C3 Bb3 F5
Can a wo - man for - get her suck - ing child that
F#m E3 A B7 E B7
Gm7 F3 Bb C7 F C3
she should not have com - pas - sion, that she should not have com -
A E3 F#m B7 Esus E
Bb3 F5 Gm7 C7 Fsus F
pas - sion on the son of her womb?
A B2 E3 C#m F#m B7 Esus E
Bb C2 F3 Dm Gm7 C7 Fsus F
Yea, they may for - get, yet will He not for - get thee. Be-
A B2 E3 C#m F#m B7 Esus E
Bb C2 F3 Dm Gm7 C7 Fsus F
hold He has grav - en thee up - on the palms of His hands.

31 Choose You This Day

Joshua 24:15

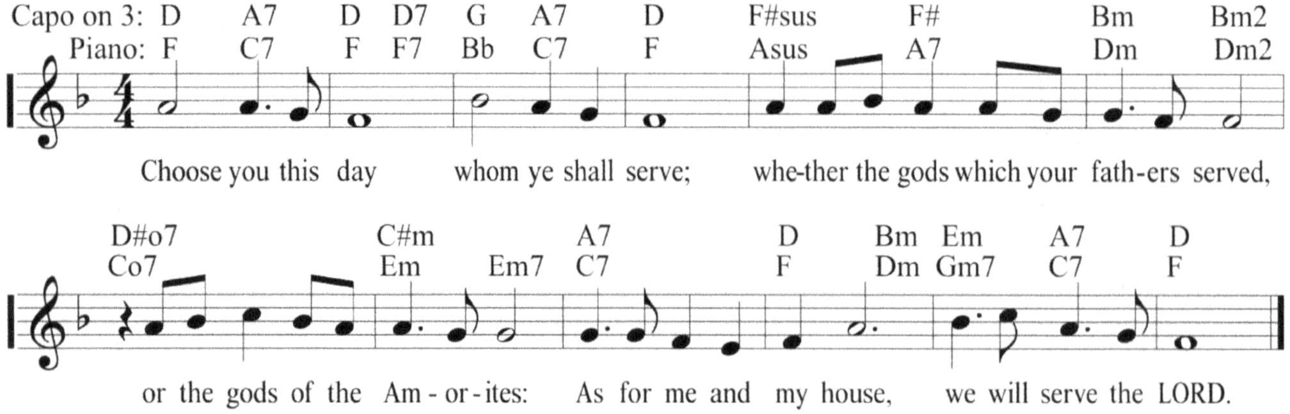
Capo on 3: D A7 D D7 G A7 D F#sus F# Bm Bm2
Piano: F C7 F F7 Bb C7 F Asus A7 Dm Dm2
Choose you this day whom ye shall serve; whe-ther the gods which your fath-ers served,
D#o7 C#m A7 D Bm Em A7 D
Co7 Em Em7 C7 F Dm Gm7 C7 F
or the gods of the Am - or - ites: As for me and my house, we will serve the LORD.

Christ in You the Hope of Glory 32
Colossians 1:26,27

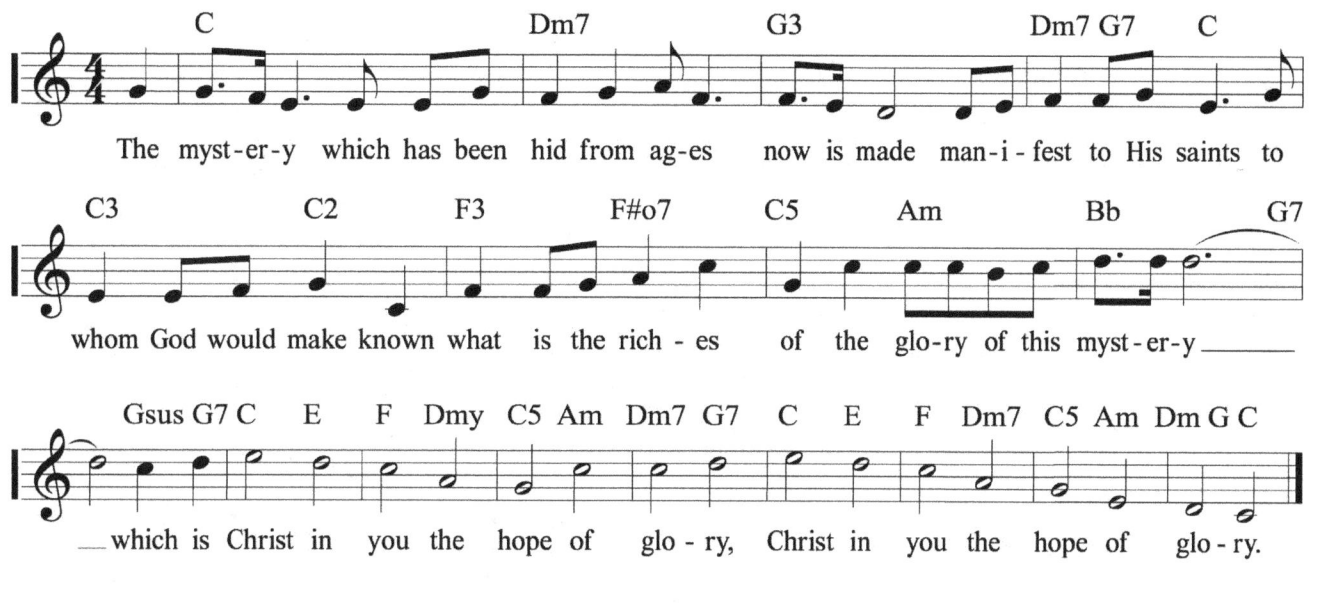

Christ Our Passover 33
1 Corinthians 5:7,8

Behold the Lamb of God which taketh away the sins of the world. John 1:29. The Lamb slain from the foundation of the world. Revelation 13:8. Forasmuch as ye know that ye were not redeemed with corruptible things, as silver and gold…but with the precious blood of Christ, as of a lamb without blemish and without spot: Who verily was foreordained before the foundation of the world. 1Peter 1:18-20.

34 Come and Let Us Go Up
Micah 4:2

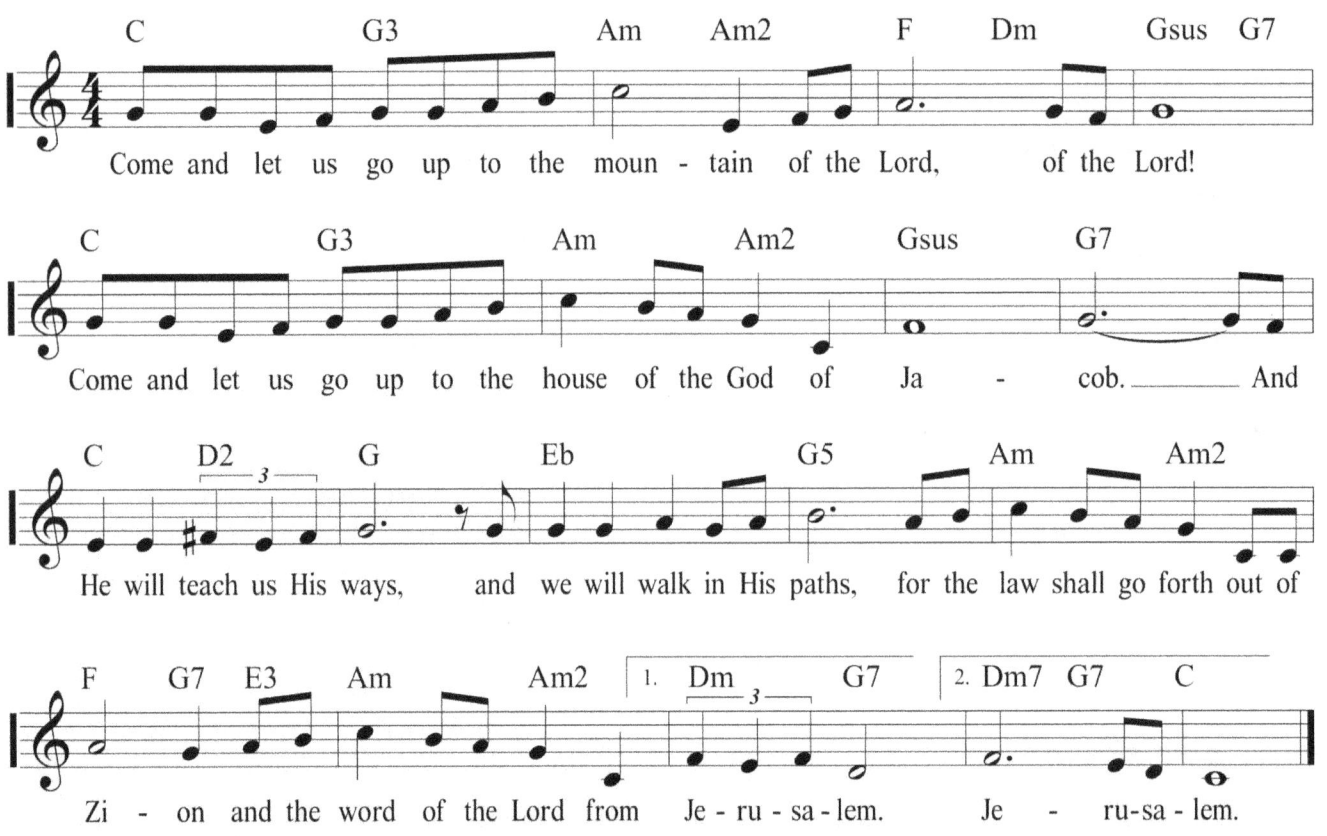

35 Come Unto Him
Matthew 11:28,29

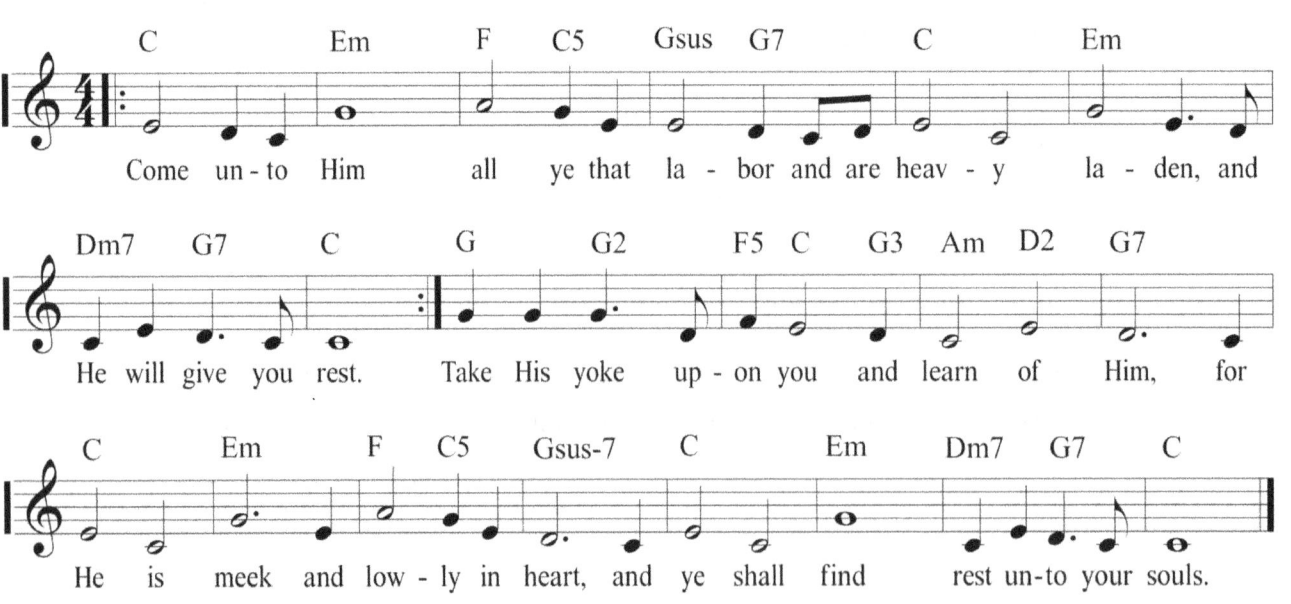

Come Ye to the Waters
Isaiah 55:1

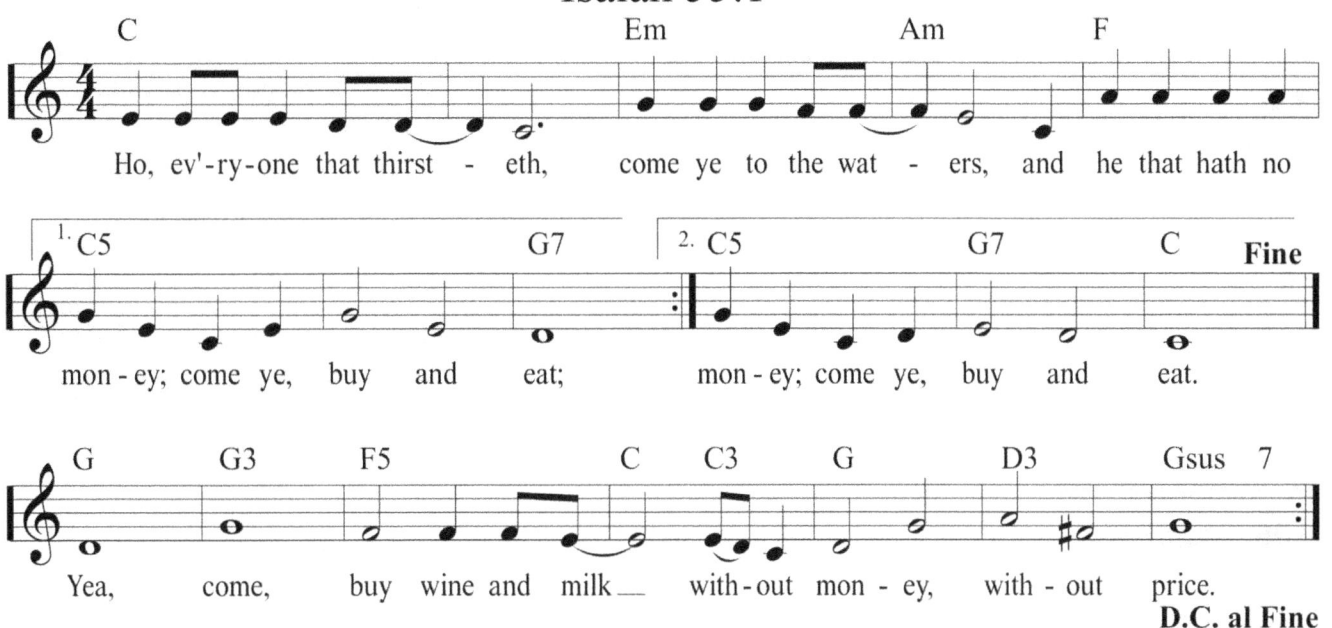

Commit Thy Way Unto the Lord
Psalm 37:5,6

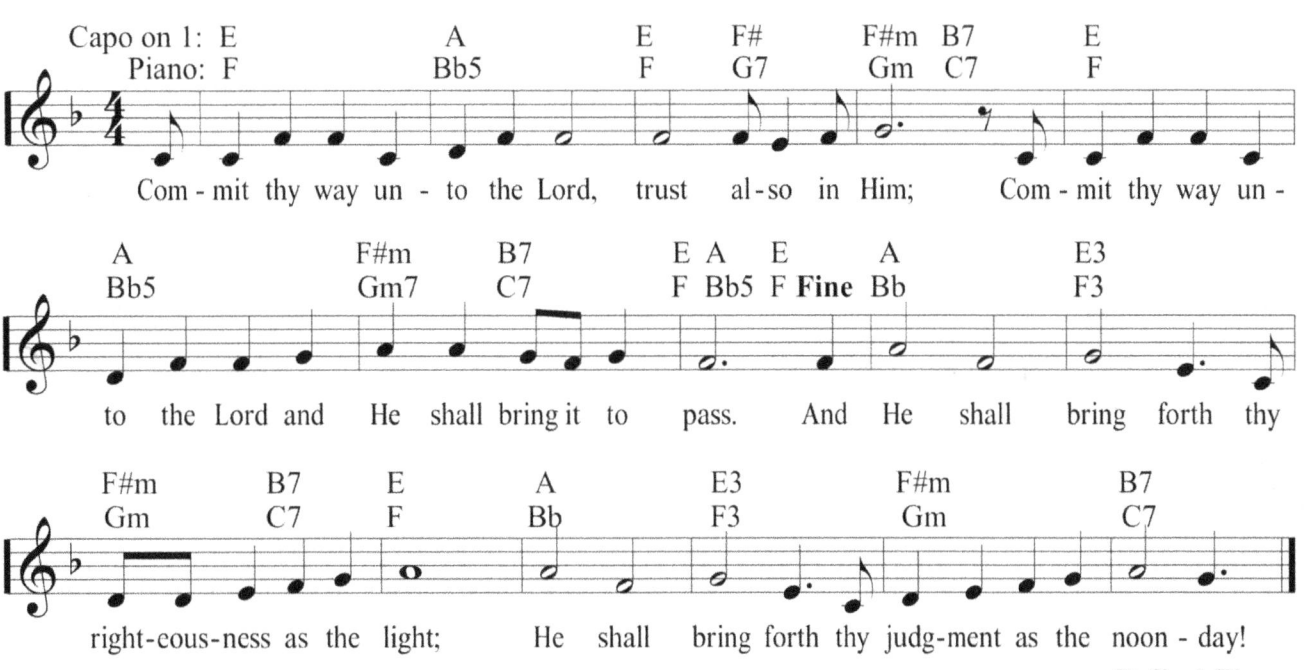

38 Count it All Joy
James 1:2-5

39 Crown of Righteousness
2 Timothy 4:8

Eye Has Not Seen
1 Corinthians 2:9

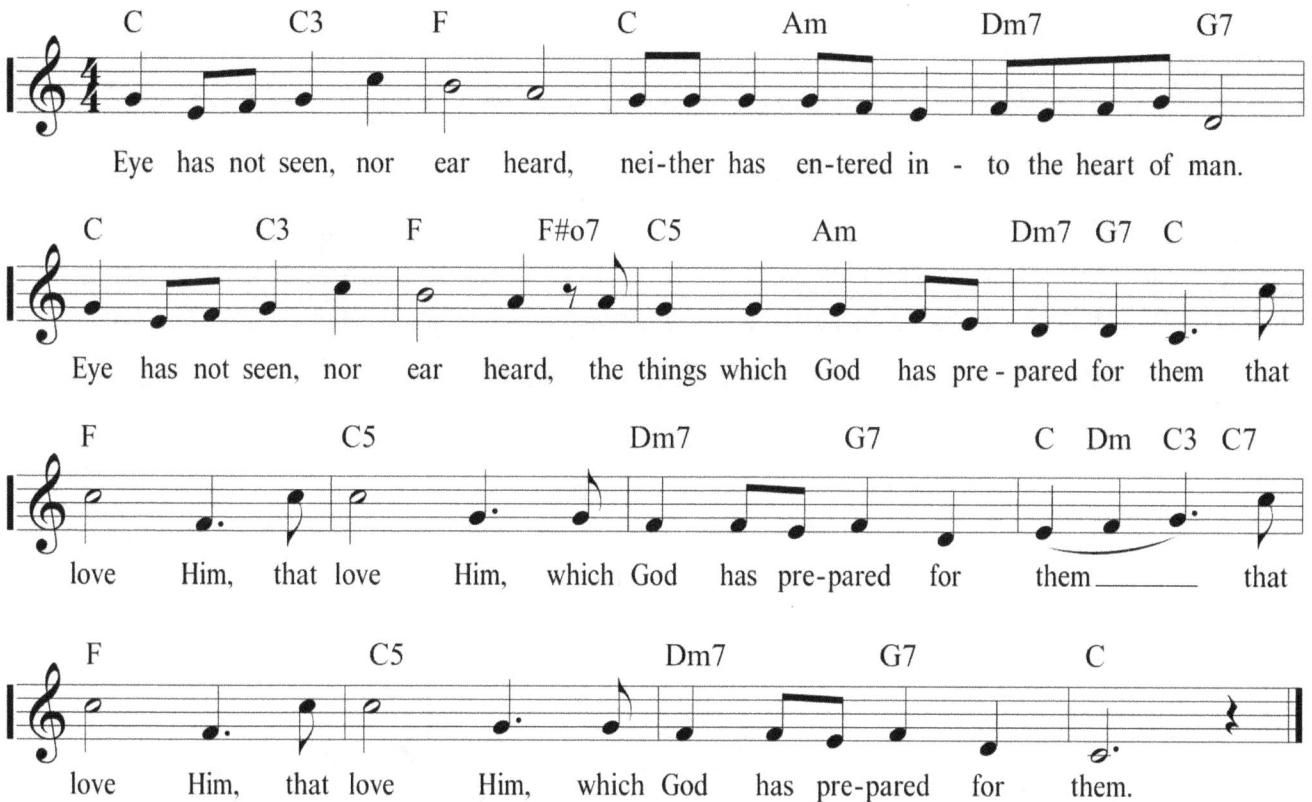

In my Father's house are many mansions: if it were not so, I would have told you. I go to prepare a place for you. And if I go and prepare a place for you, I will come again, and receive you unto myself; that where I am, there ye may be also. John 14:2,3. The wolf also shall dwell with the lamb, and the leopard shall lie down with the kid; and the calf and the young lion and the fatling together; and a little child shall lead them…They shall not hurt nor destroy in all my holy mountain. Isaiah 11:6,9. And they shall build houses, and inhabit them; and they shall plant vineyards, and eat the fruit of them. They shall not build, and another inhabit; they shall not plant, and another eat. Isaiah 65:21,22. And there shall be no night there; and they need no candle, neither light of the sun; for the Lord God giveth them light: and they shall reign for ever and ever. Revelation 22:5.

41 Fear God and Give Glory to Him
Revelation 14:6,7,12

And I looked, and behold a white cloud, and upon the cloud one sat like unto the Son of man, having on his head a golden crown, and in his hand a sharp sickle. And another angel came out of the temple, crying with a loud voice to him that sat on the cloud, Thrust in thy sickle, and reap: for the time is come for thee to reap; for the harvest of the earth is ripe. Revelation 14:14,15.

Fear Thou Not 42

Isaiah 41:10

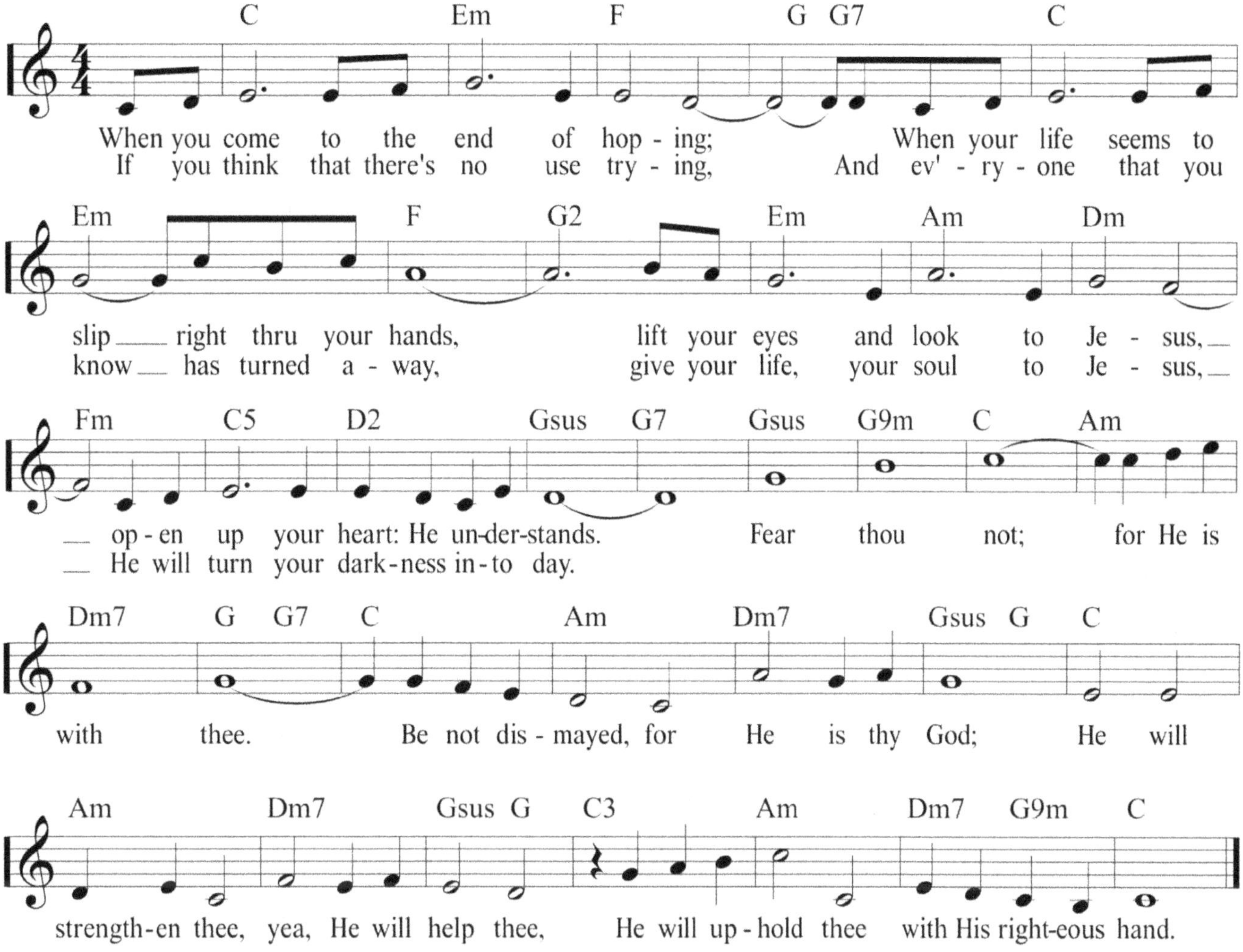
C Em F G G7 C
When you come to the end of hop - ing; When your life seems to
If you think that there's no use try - ing, And ev' - ry - one that you
Em F G2 Em Am Dm
slip right thru your hands, lift your eyes and look to Je - sus,
know has turned a - way, give your life, your soul to Je - sus,
Fm C5 D2 Gsus G7 Gsus G9m C Am
op - en up your heart: He un-der-stands. Fear thou not; for He is
He will turn your dark-ness in-to day.
Dm7 G G7 C Am Dm7 Gsus G C
with thee. Be not dis - mayed, for He is thy God; He will
Am Dm7 Gsus G C3 Am Dm7 G9m C
strength-en thee, yea, He will help thee, He will up - hold thee with His right-eous hand.

For God So Loved This Little World 43

John 3:16 adapted

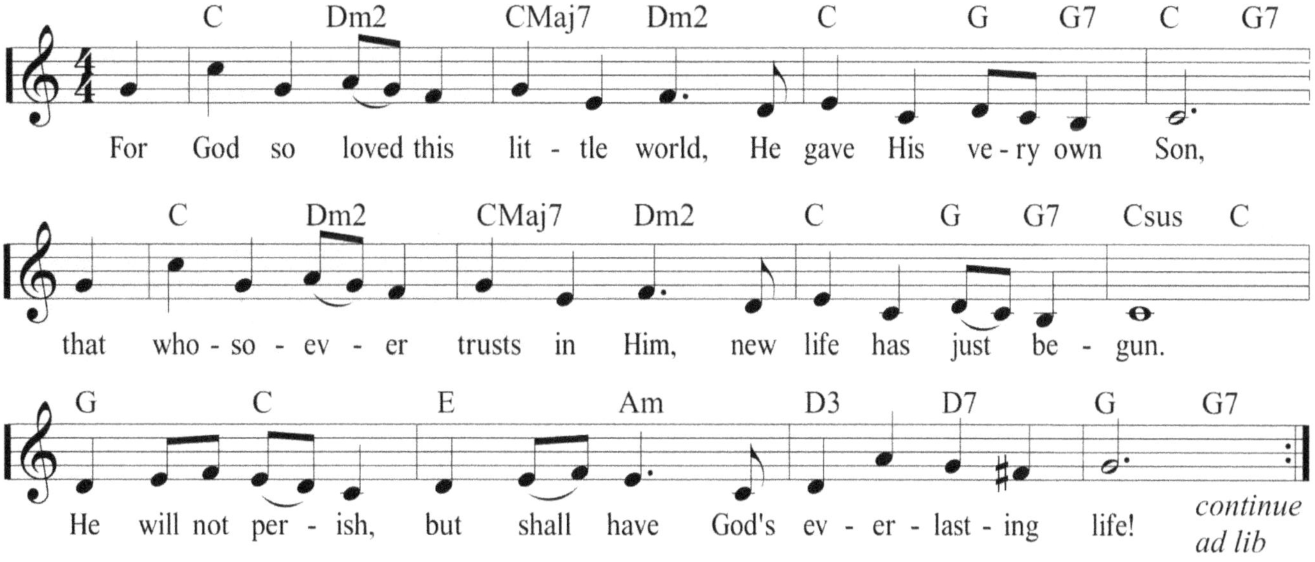
C Dm2 CMaj7 Dm2 C G G7 C G7
For God so loved this lit - tle world, He gave His ve - ry own Son,
C Dm2 CMaj7 Dm2 C G G7 Csus C
that who - so - ev - er trusts in Him, new life has just be - gun.
G C E Am D3 D7 G G7
He will not per - ish, but shall have God's ev - er - last - ing life!
continue ad lib

44 From Glory to Glory
2 Corinthians 3:18

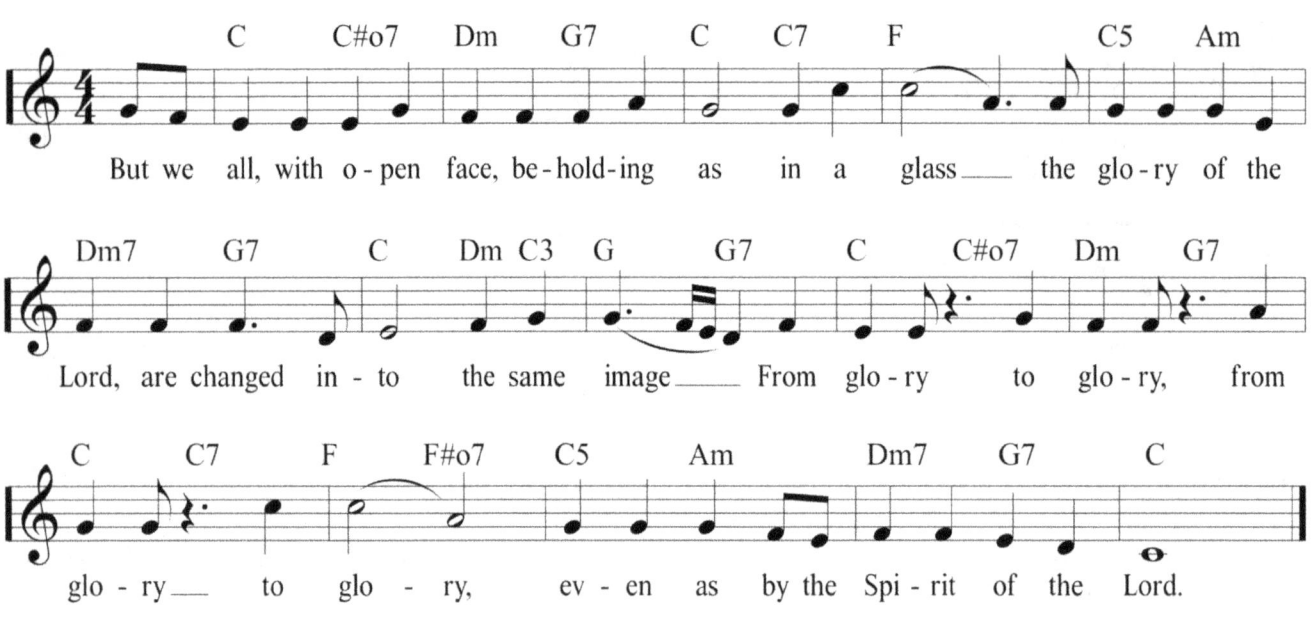

45 Fruit of the Spirit
Galatians 5:22,23

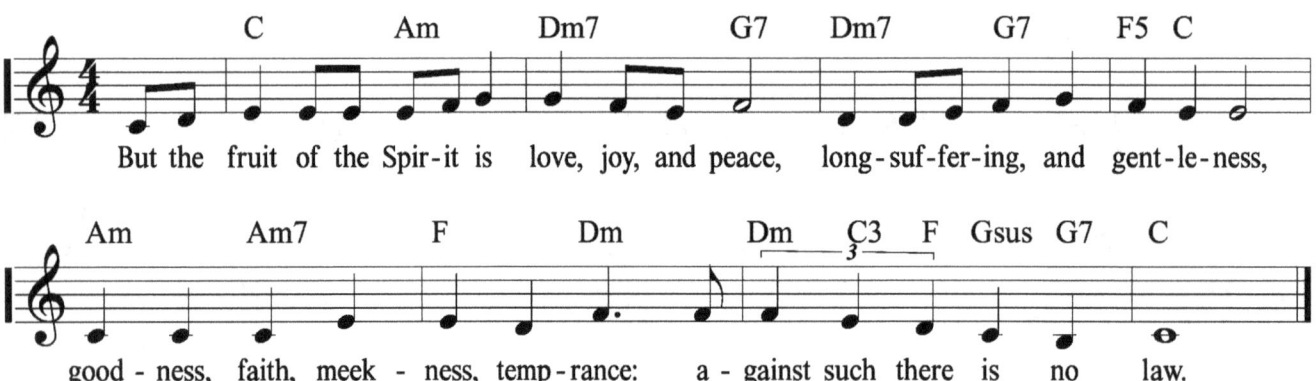

Follow after righteousness, godliness, faith, love, patience, meekness. Fight the good fight of faith, lay hold on eternal life, whereunto thou art also called, and hast professed a good profession before many witnesses. I give thee charge in the sight of God, who quickeneth all things, and before Christ Jesus…that thou keep this commandment without spot, unrebukable, until the appearing of our Lord Jesus Christ. 1 Timothy 6:11-14.

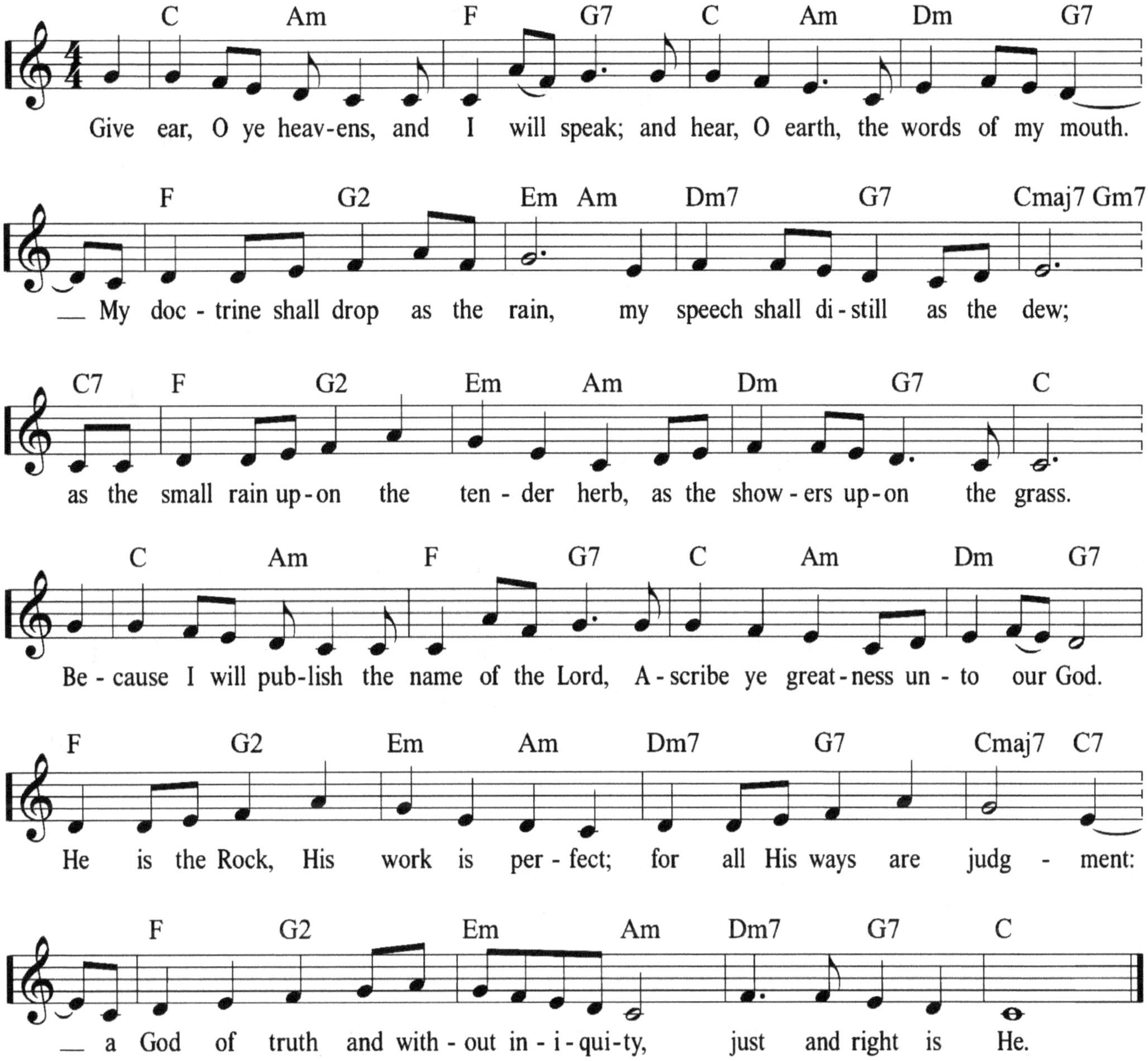

Give Ear O Ye Heavens 46

Deuteronomy 32:1-4

C Am F G7 C Am Dm G7
Give ear, O ye heav-ens, and I will speak; and hear, O earth, the words of my mouth.
F G2 Em Am Dm7 G7 Cmaj7 Gm7
— My doc-trine shall drop as the rain, my speech shall di-still as the dew;
C7 F G2 Em Am Dm G7 C
as the small rain up-on the ten-der herb, as the show-ers up-on the grass.
C Am F G7 C Am Dm G7
Be-cause I will pub-lish the name of the Lord, A-scribe ye great-ness un-to our God.
F G2 Em Am Dm7 G7 Cmaj7 C7
He is the Rock, His work is per-fect; for all His ways are judg-ment:
F G2 Em Am Dm7 G7 C
— a God of truth and with-out in-i-qui-ty, just and right is He.

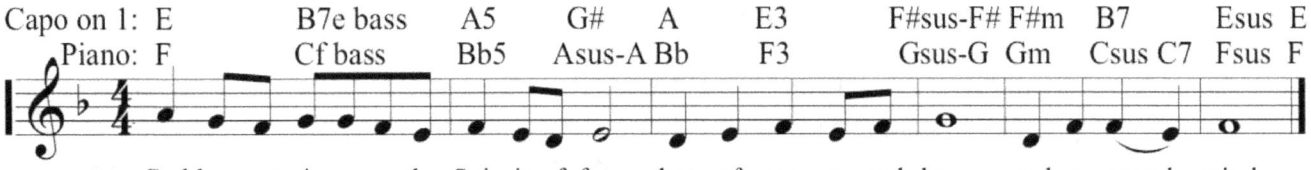

God Has Not Given Us 47

2 Timothy 1:7

Capo on 1: E B7e bass A5 G# A E3 F#sus-F# F#m B7 Esus E
Piano: F Cf bass Bb5 Asus-A Bb F3 Gsus-G Gm Csus C7 Fsus F
God has not giv-en us the Spir-it of fear, but of pow-er and love, and a sound mind.

48 God Hath Sent the Spirit
Galatians 4:6

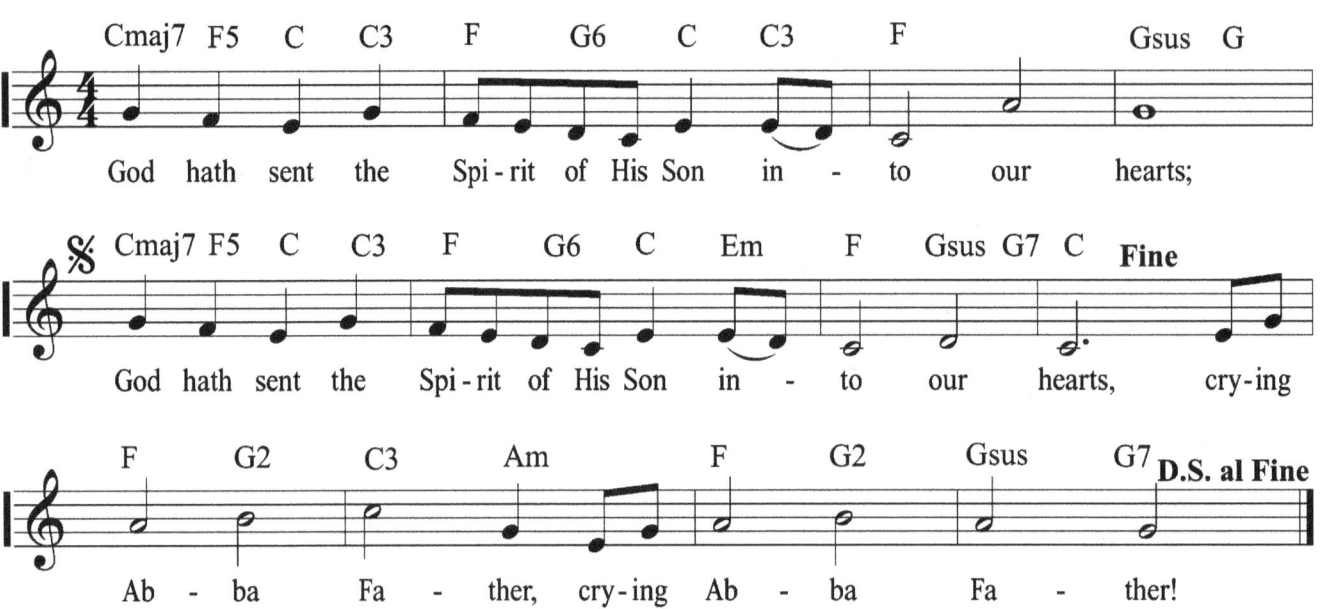

Know ye not your own selves how that Jesus Christ is in you? 2Corinthians 13:5. What? Know ye not that your body is the temple of the Holy Spirit which is in you? 1Corinthains 6:19. Now if any man hath not the Spirit of Christ, he is none of His. And if Christ be in you…the Spirit is life. Romans 8:9,10. This mystery among the Gentiles; which is Christ in you, the hope of glory. Colossians 1:27.

49 God is My Salvation
Isaiah 12:2,3

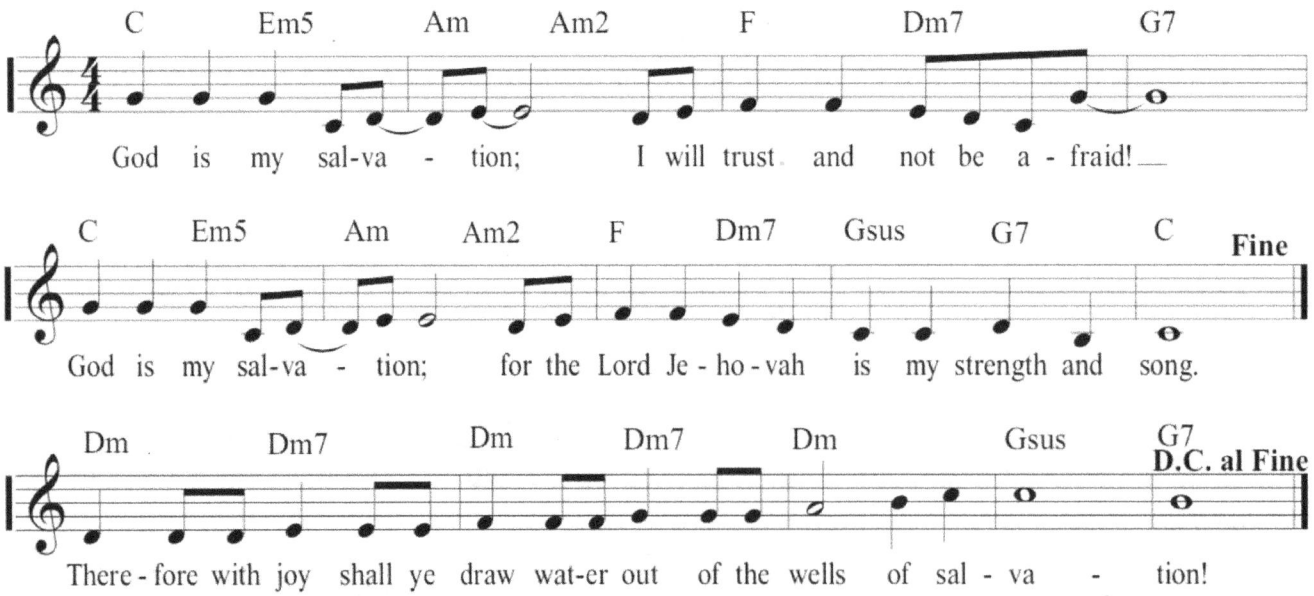

God is Our Refuge
Psalm 46:1-3

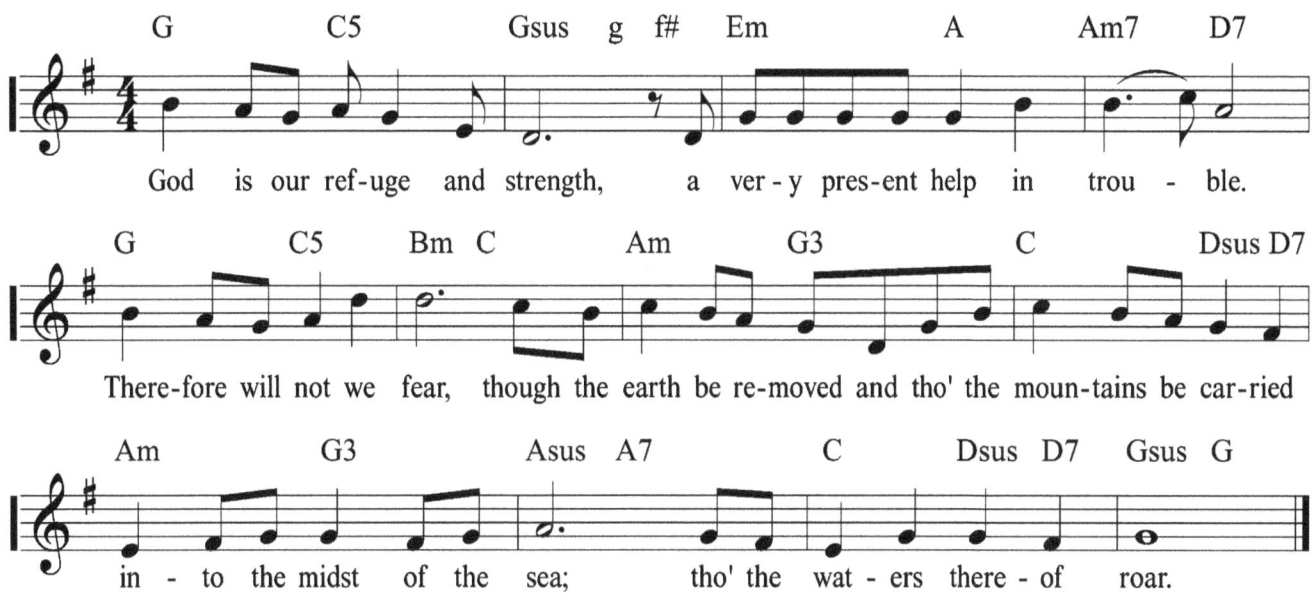

God of This World
2 Corinthians 4:4,5

In time past ye walked according to the course of this world, according to the prince of the power of the air, the spirit that now worketh in the children of disobedience…and were by nature the children of wrath, even as others. But God who is rich in mercy, for His great love wherewith He loved us, even when we were dead in sins, hath quickened us together with Christ, and hath raised us up together, and made us sit together in heavenly places: that in the ages yet to come He might shew the exceeding riches of His grace in His kindness toward us through Christ Jesus. Ephesians 2:2-7

52 God Who Commanded the Light
2 Corinthians 4:6

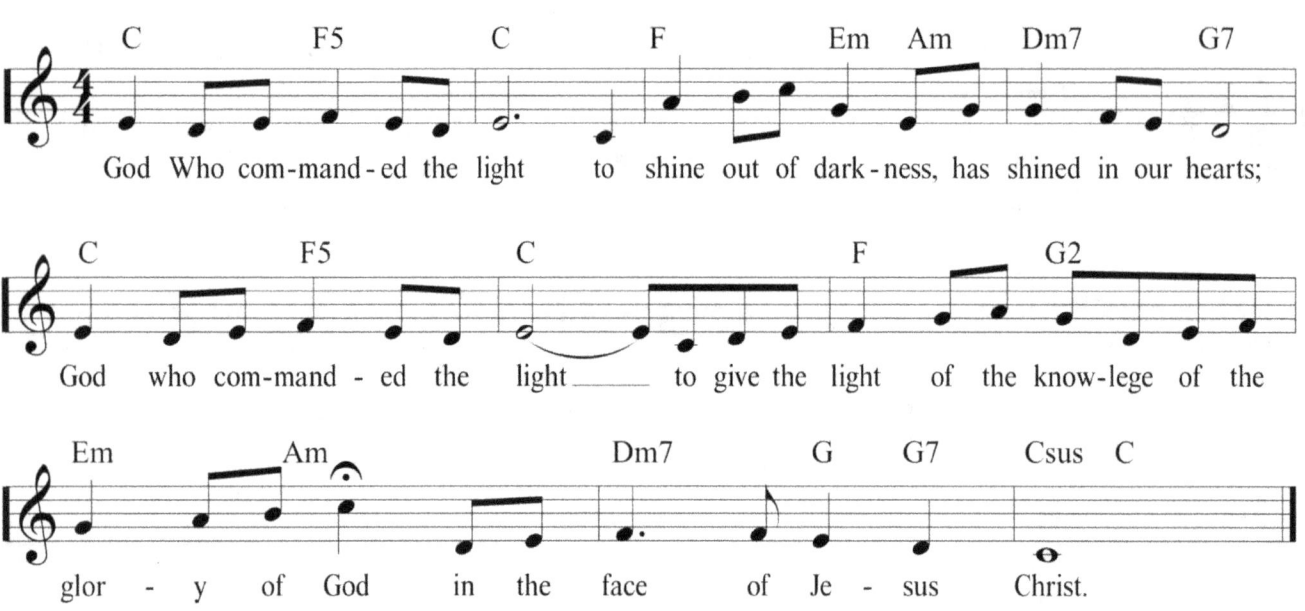

And God said, Let there be light: and there was light. And God saw the light, that it was good. Genesis 1:3,4. And the light shineth in darkness; and the darkness comprehended it not…That was the true Light, which lighteth every man that cometh into the world. John 1:5,9.

53 Grace Be to You
2 John 3

Great and Marvellous

Song of Moses and the Lamb

Revelation 15:3,4

Hallelu Jah

Psalm 68:4

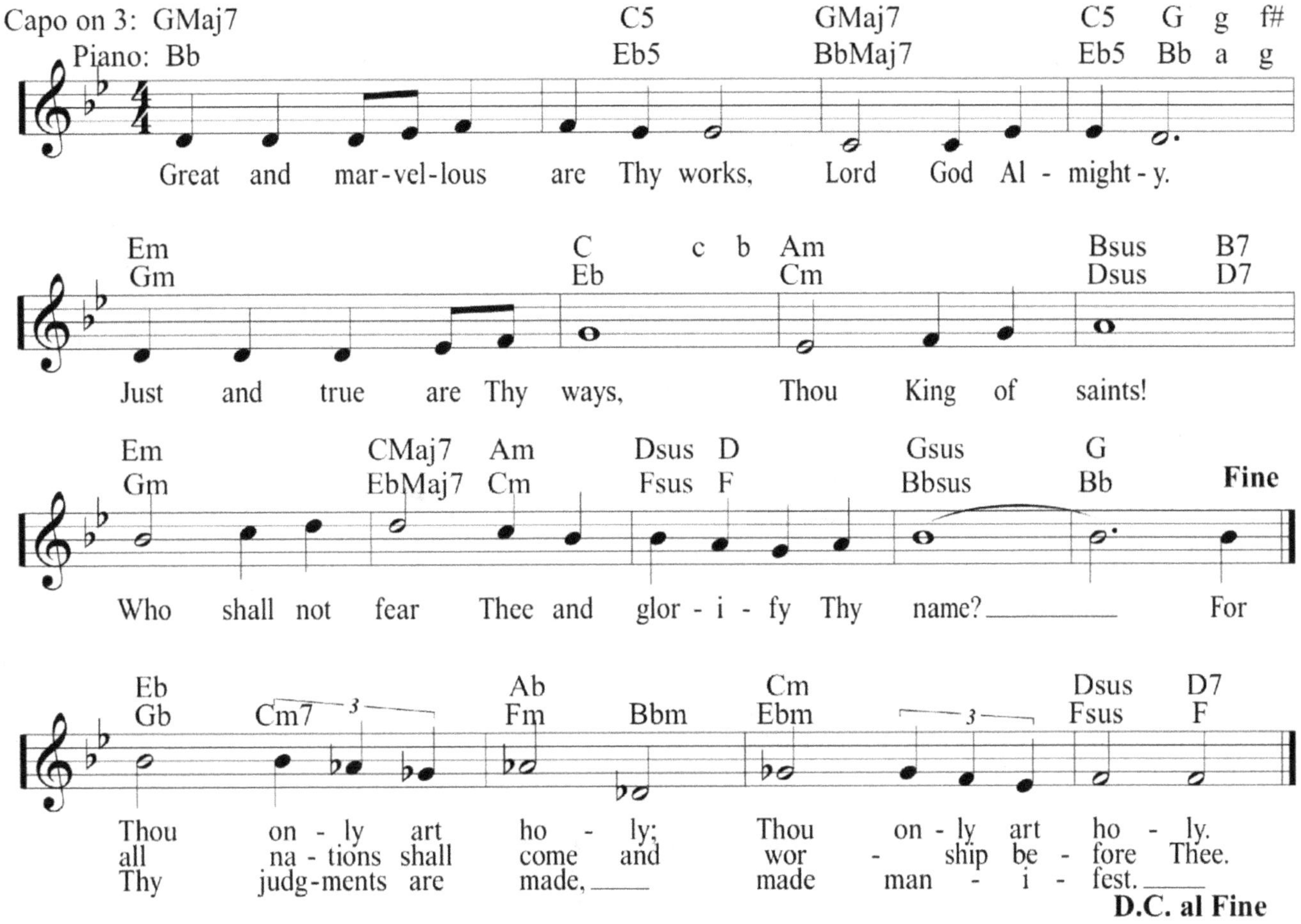

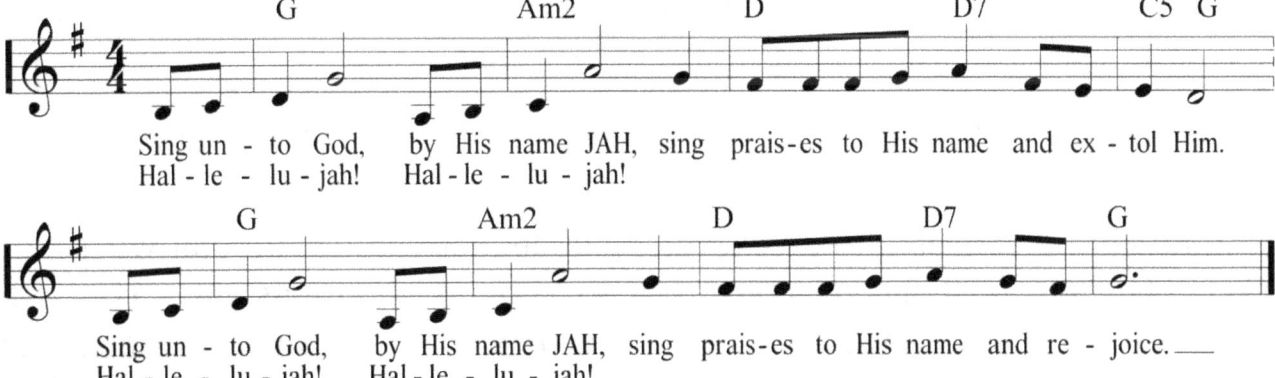

56 He Has Blotted Out
Isaiah 44:22

57 He is Able Also To
Hebrews 7:25

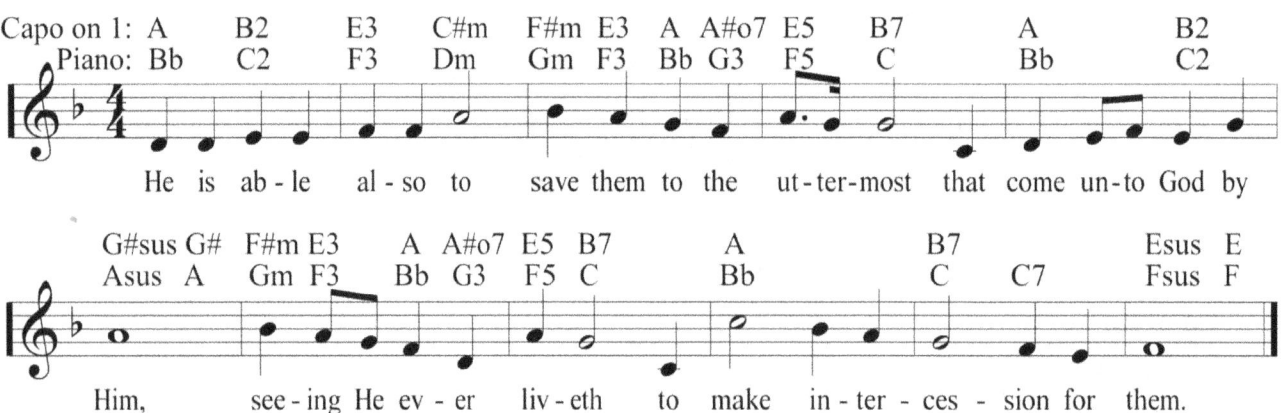

Now unto Him that is able to do exceeding abundantly above all that we ask or think. Ephesians 3:20. He is able even to subdue all things unto Himself. Philippians 3:21. I know in whom I have believed, and am persuaded that He is able to keep that which I have committed unto Him against that day. 2Timothy 1:12.

He That Dwelleth 58

Psalm 91:1,2

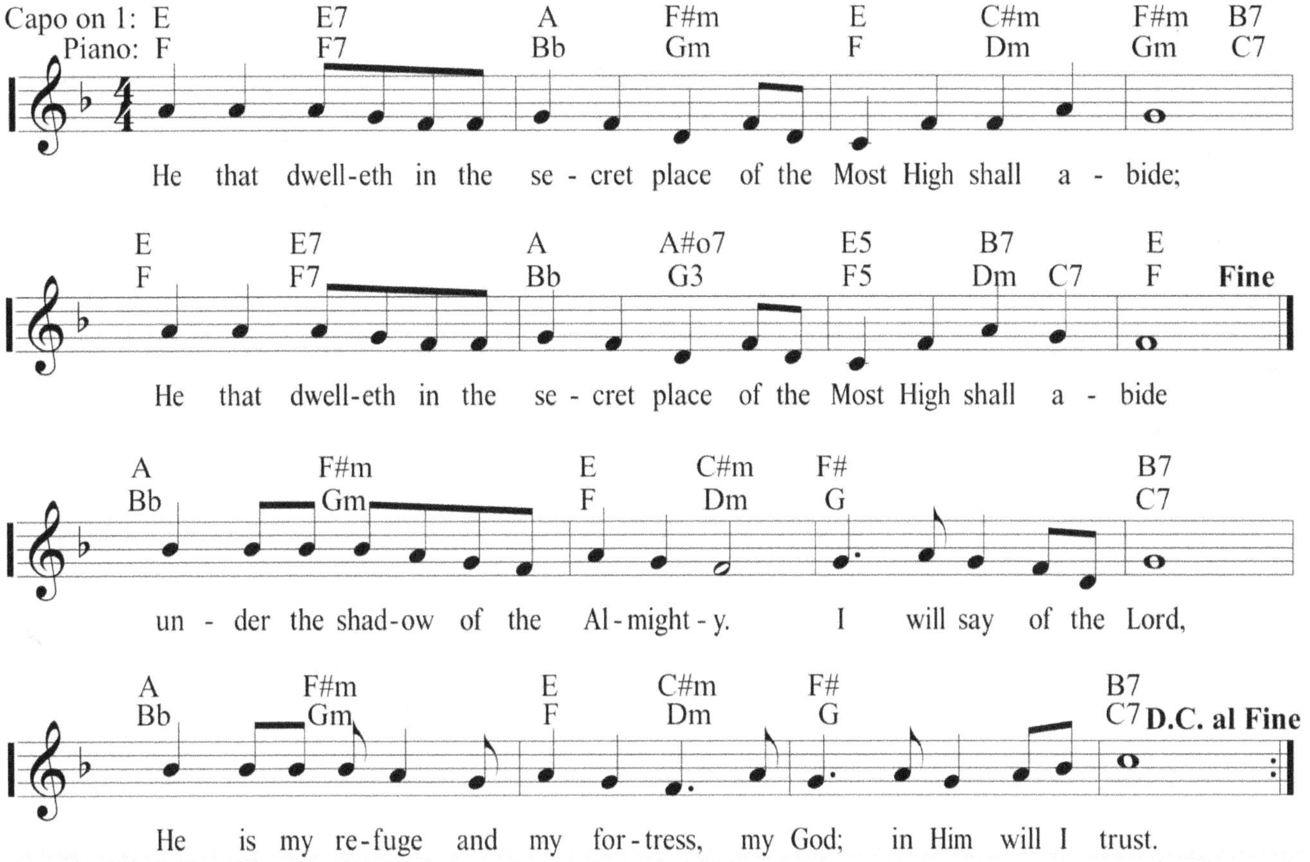
Capo on 1: E E7 A F#m E C#m F#m B7
Piano: F F7 Bb Gm F Dm Gm C7
He that dwell-eth in the se - cret place of the Most High shall a - bide;
E E7 A A#o7 E5 B7 E
F F7 Bb G3 F5 Dm C7 F Fine
He that dwell-eth in the se - cret place of the Most High shall a - bide
A F#m E C#m F# B7
Bb Gm F Dm G C7
un - der the shad-ow of the Al-might - y. I will say of the Lord,
A F#m E C#m F# B7
Bb Gm F Dm G C7 D.C. al Fine
He is my re-fuge and my for-tress, my God; in Him will I trust.

He That Spared Not His Own Son 59

Romans 8:32; John 3:35; Hebrews 1:2

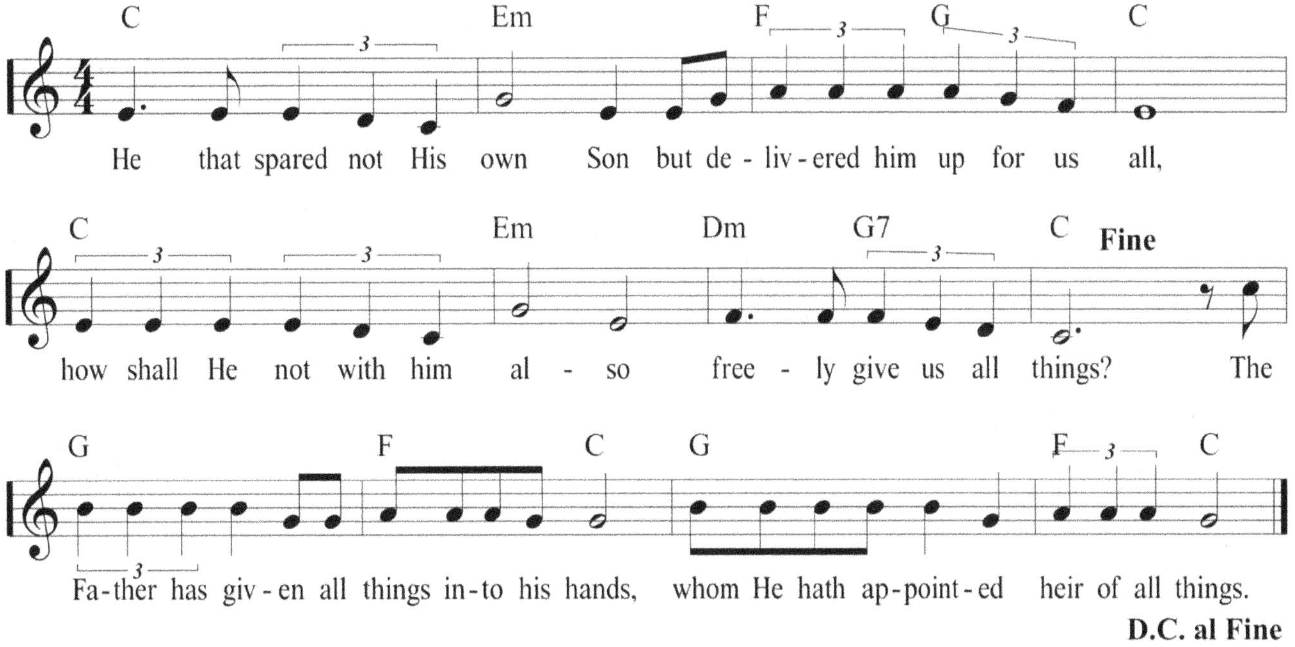
C Em F G C
He that spared not His own Son but de - liv-ered him up for us all,
C Em Dm G7 C Fine
how shall He not with him al - so free - ly give us all things? The
G F C G F C
Fa-ther has giv-en all things in-to his hands, whom He hath ap-point-ed heir of all things.
D.C. al Fine

60 He Whom God Hath Sent
John 3:34,35

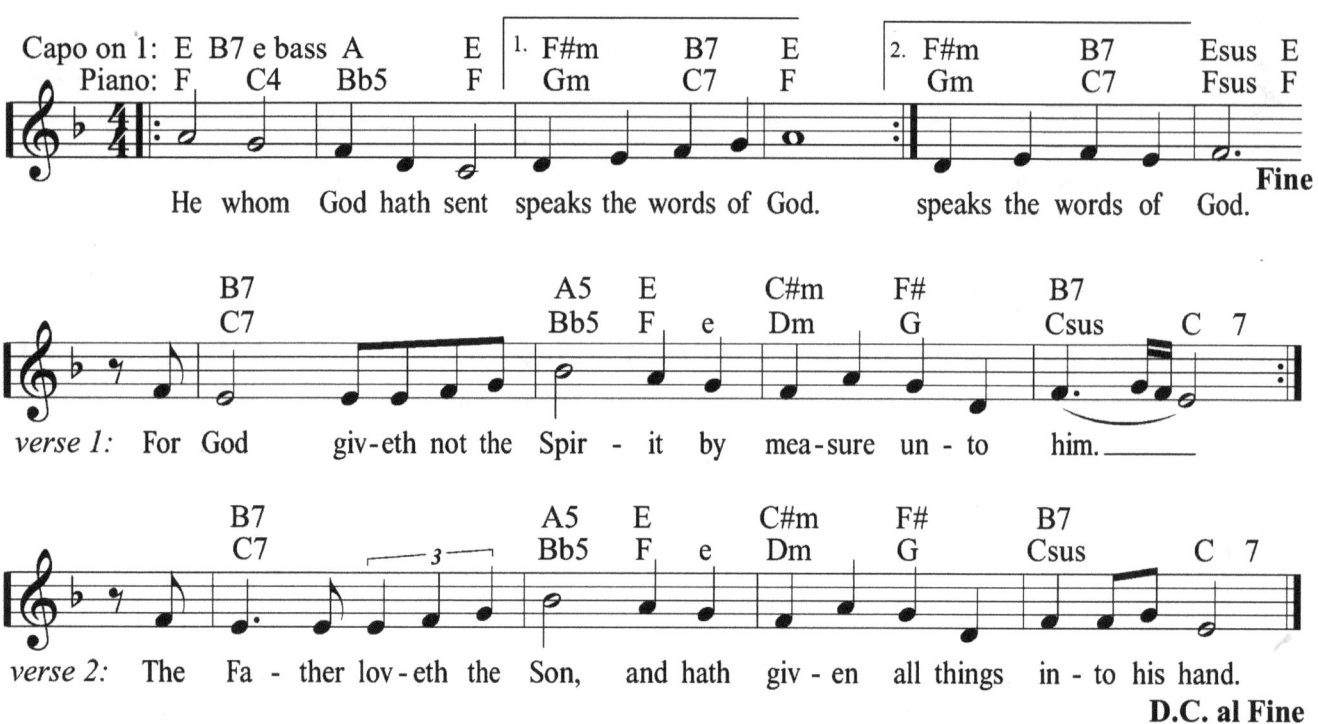

61 He Will Never Leave You
Hebrews 13:5; Matthew 28:20; 2 Corinthians 13:5

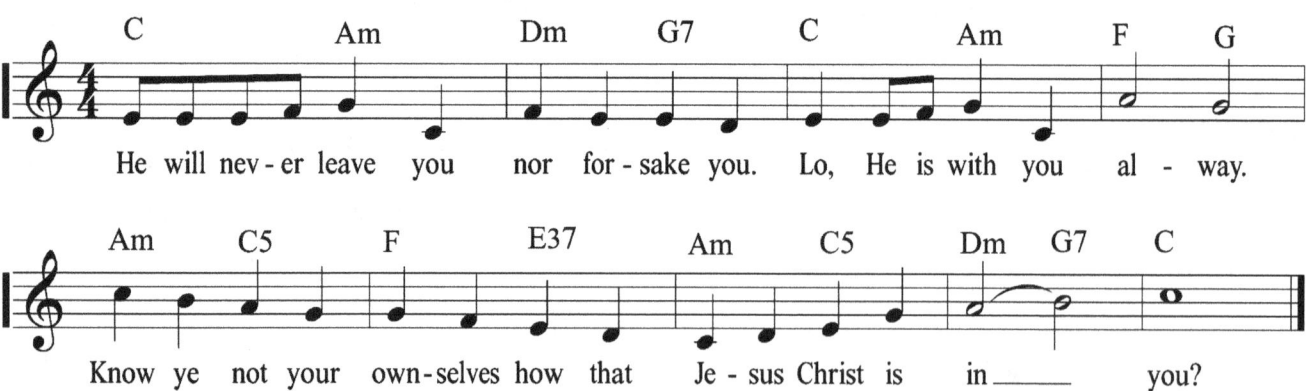

I will not leave you comfortless: I will come to you. John 14:18. The Lord be with you all. 2Thessalonians 3:16. For the LORD thy God is a merciful God; He will not forsake thee, neither destroy thee, nor forget the covenant of thy fathers which he sware unto them. Deuteronomy 4:31.

Heal Me, O Lord
Jeremiah 17:14

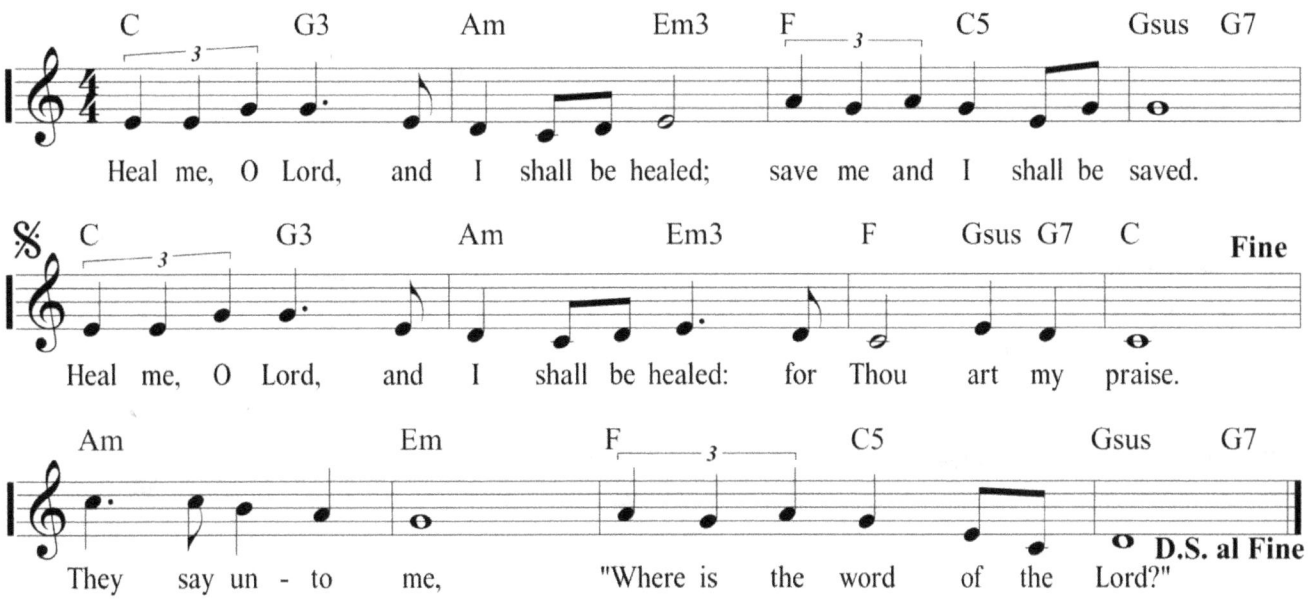

High and Lofty One
Isaiah 57:14,15

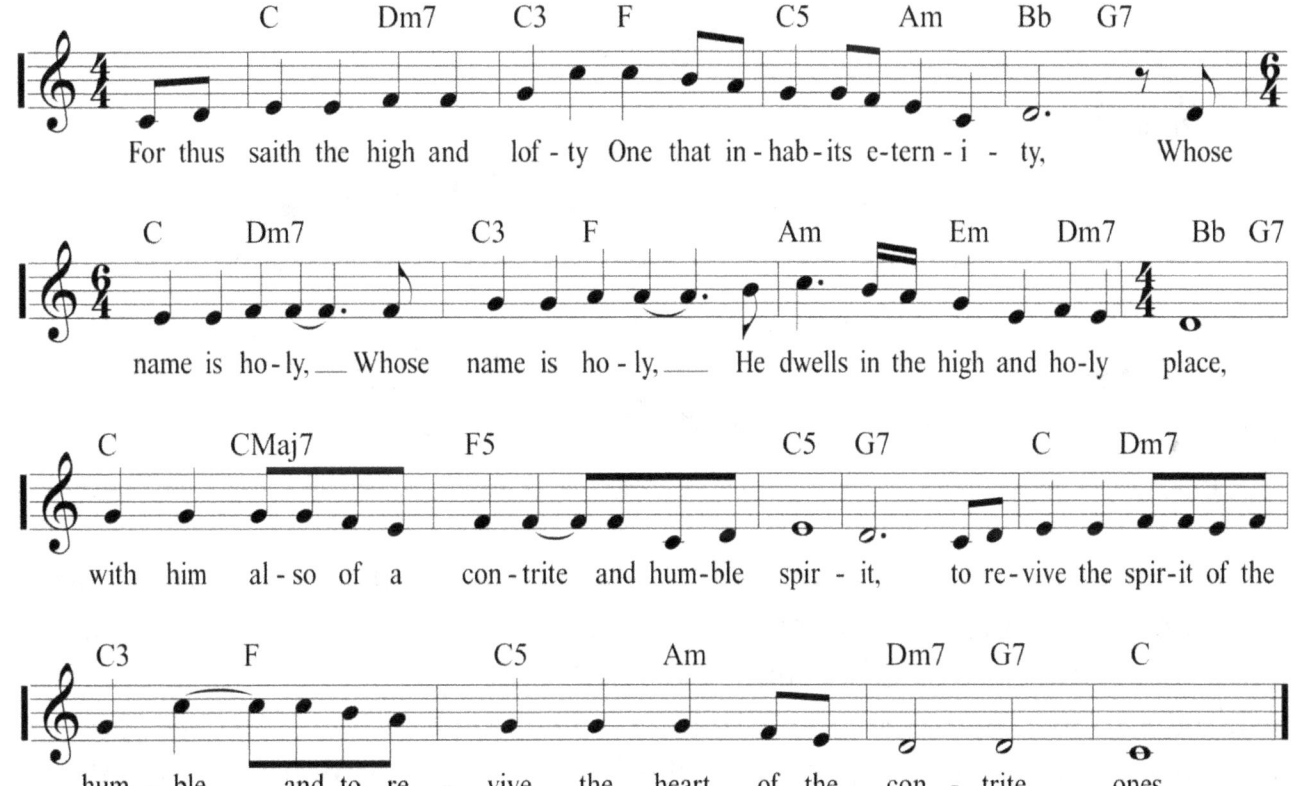

64 Him That Overcometh
Revelation 3:12

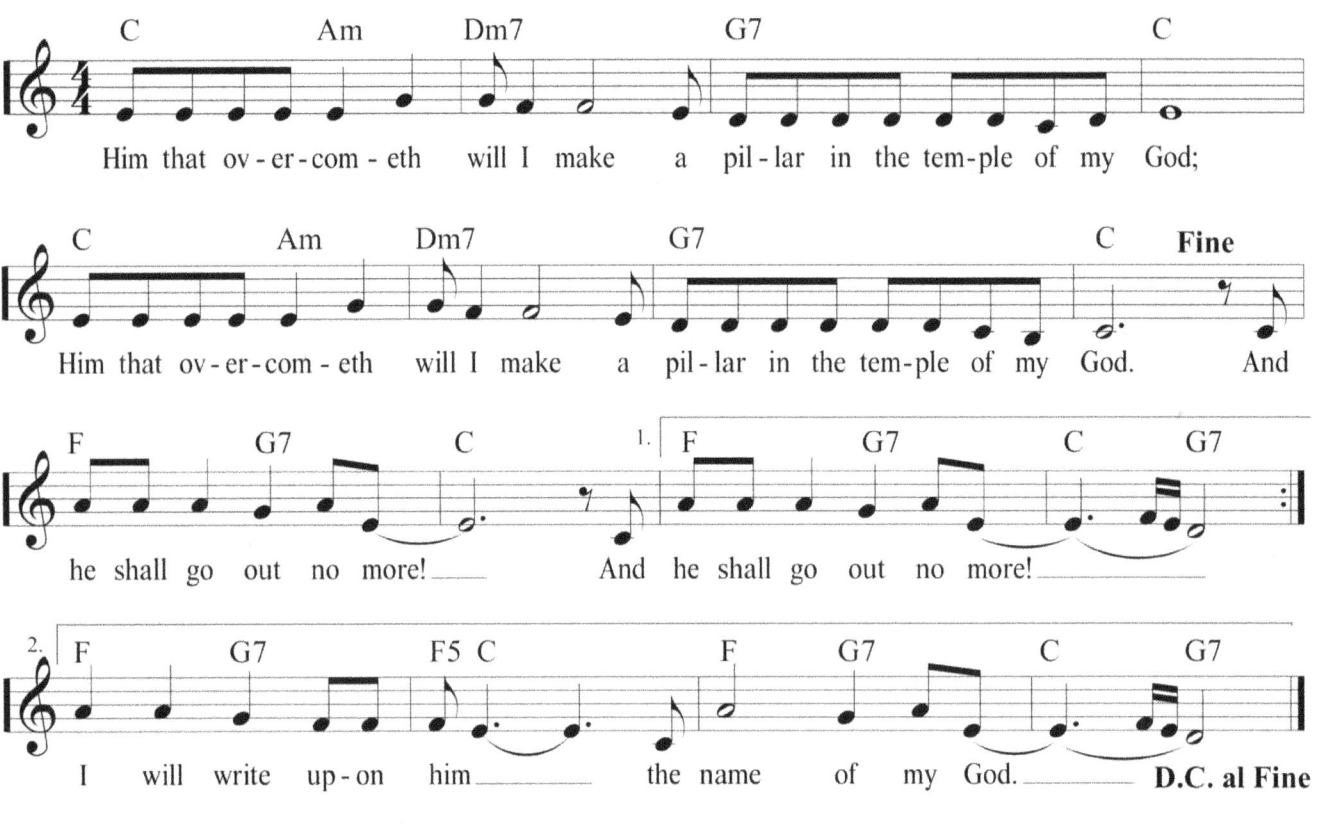

65 Hour Cometh and Now Is
John 4:23

God is a Spirit: and they that worship Him must worship Him in spirit and in truth. John 4:24. Worship Him that made heaven, and earth, and the fountains of waters. Revelation 14:7. Give unto the LORD the glory due unto His name; worship the LORD in the beauty of holiness. The voice of the LORD is upon the waters: the God of glory thundereth: the LORD is upon many waters. Psalm 29:2,3. And the Spirit of God moved upon the face of the waters. Genesis 1:2.

How Long Halt Ye? 66
1 Kings 18:21

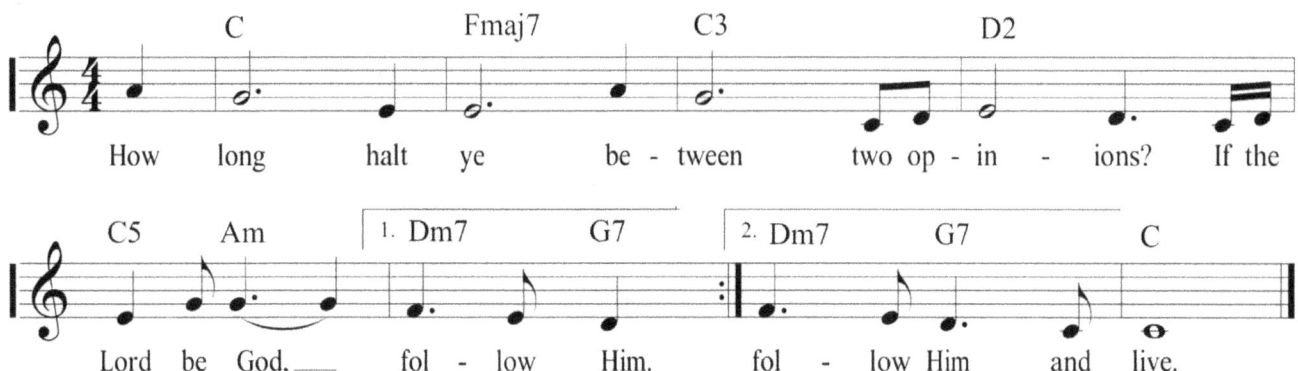

Multitudes, multitudes in the valley of decision: for the day of the LORD is near in the valley of decision. Joel 3:14. Choose you this day whom ye will serve. Joshua 24:15.

But Christ being come an high priest of good things to come…Neither by the blood of goats and calves, but by his own blood he entered in once into the holy place, having obtained eternal redemption for us. Hebrews 9:11,12.

How Much More? 67
Hebrews 9:14

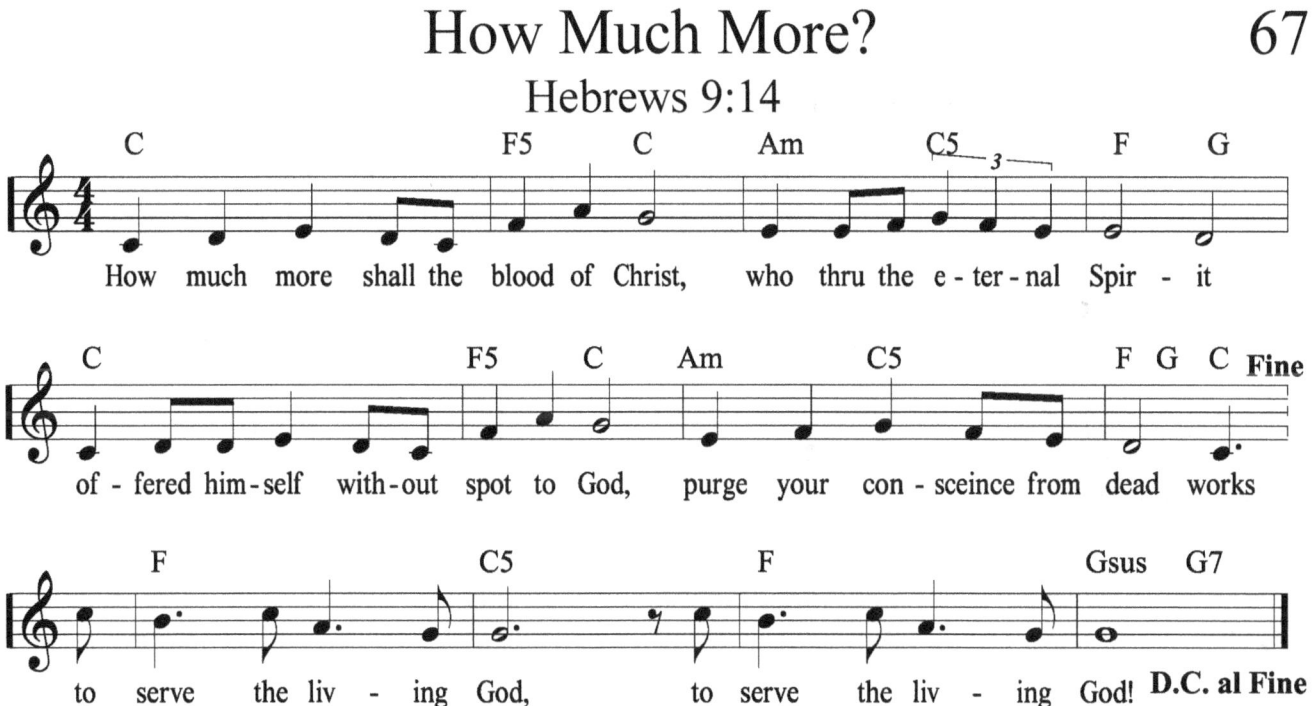

68 How Pleasant It Is
Psalm 133

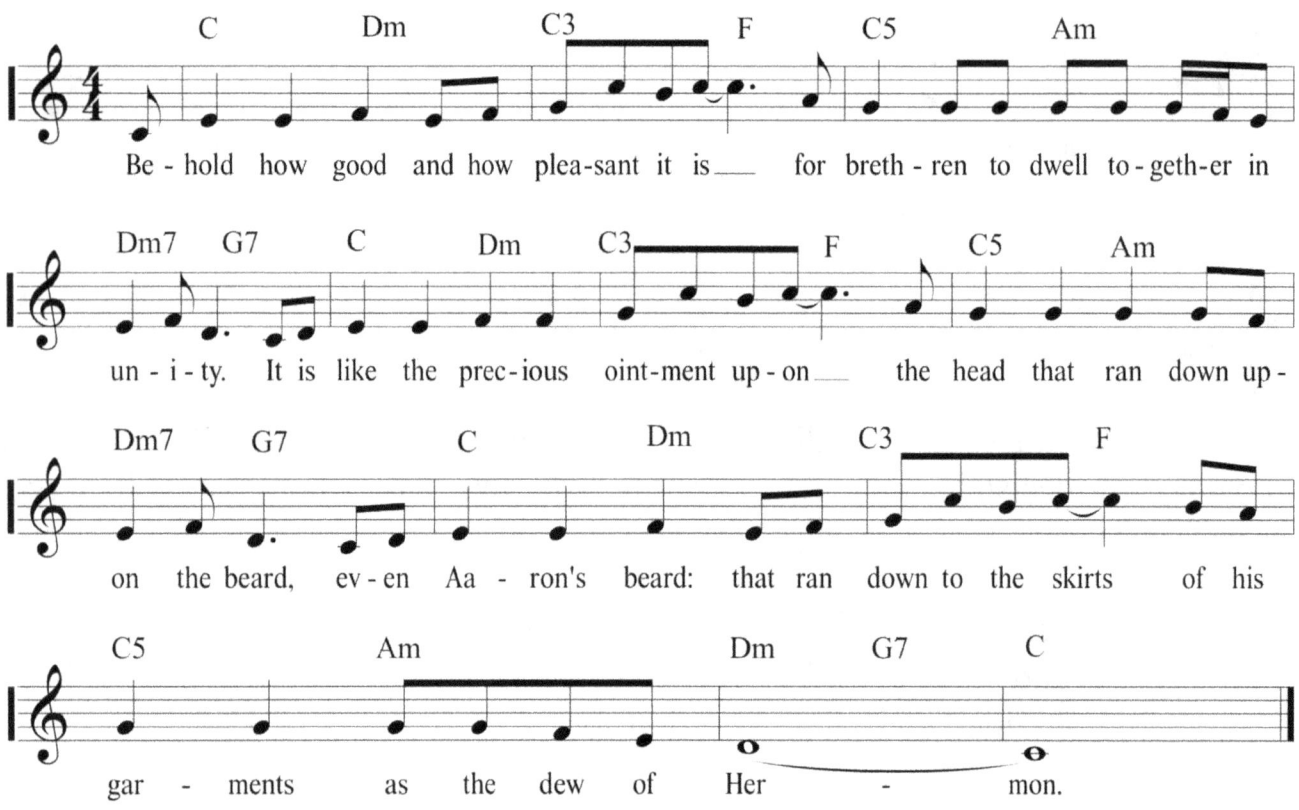

69 Humble Yourselves
1 Peter 5:6,7

I Am Not Ashamed 70

Romans 1:16

I Beseech You Therefore Brethren 71

Romans 12:1,2

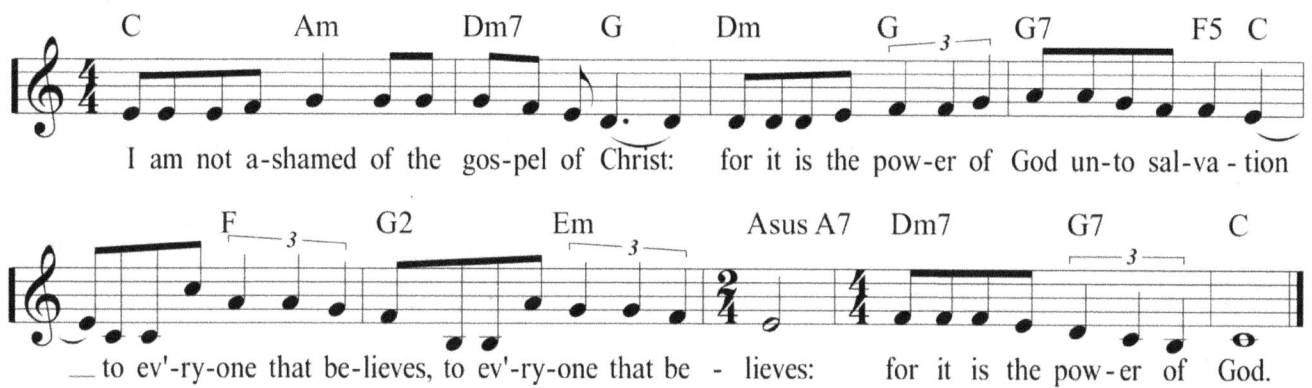

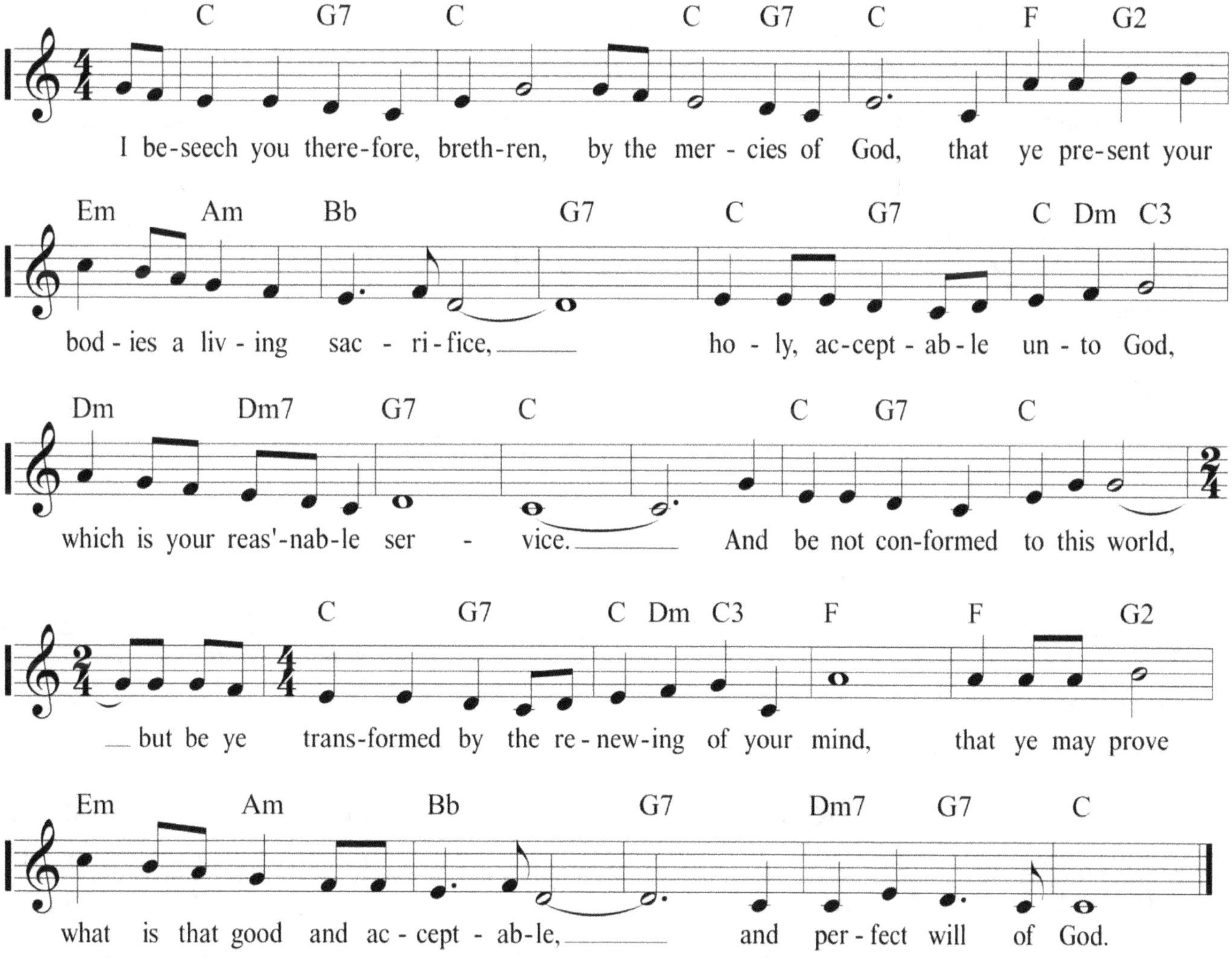

72   I Bow My Knees
Ephesians 3:14-19

That their hearts might be comforted, being knit together in love, and unto all riches of the full assurance of understanding, to the acknowledgement of the mystery of God, and of the Father, and of Christ; in whom are hid all the treasures of wisdom and knowledge…For in him dwelleth all the fulness of the Godhead bodily. Colossians 2:2,3,9.

I Charge Thee Before God
1 Timothy 5:21

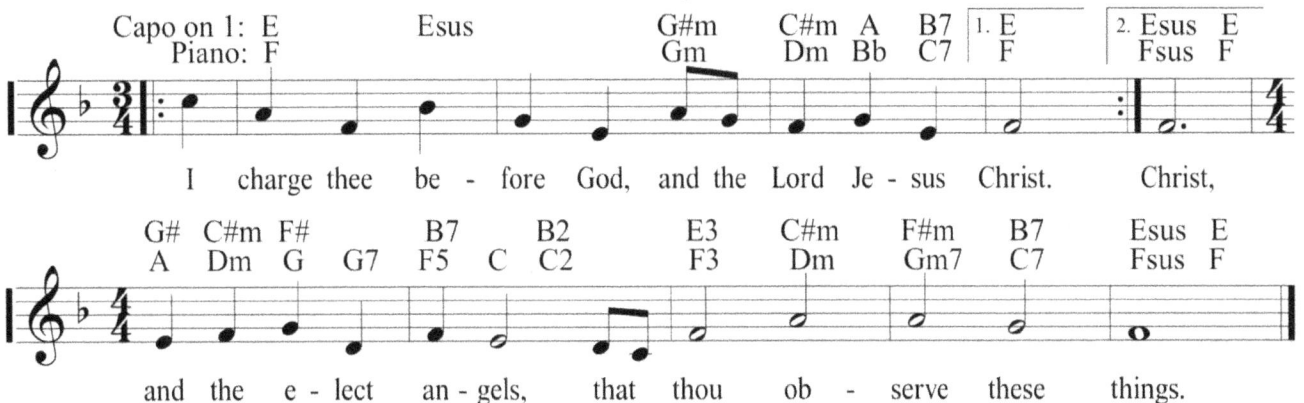

I Gave Them My Statutes
Ezekiel 20:11,12

The law of the LORD is perfect, converting the soul;
The testimony of the LORD is sure, making wise the simple.
The statutes of the LORD are right, rejoicing the heart:
The commandment of the LORD is pure, enlightening the eyes. Psalm 19:7,8.

75   I Send an Angel
Exodus 23:20,21

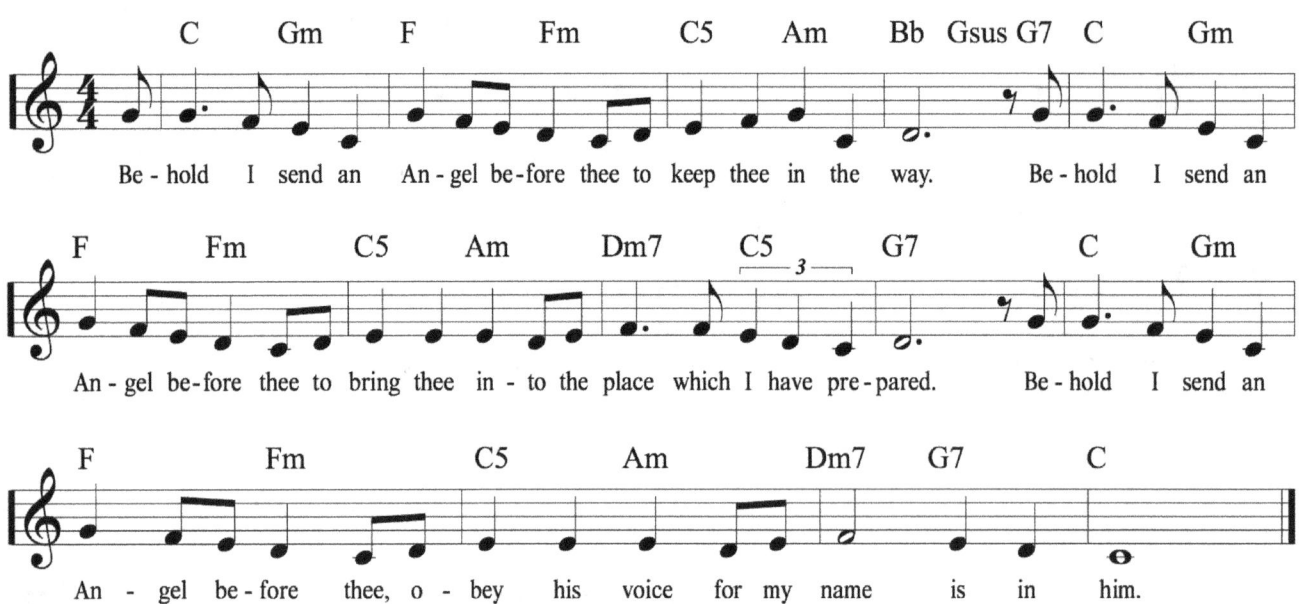

I am come in my Father's name. John 5:43. The works that I do in my Father's name, they bear witness of me. John 10:25. Wherefore God also hath…given him a name which is above every name. Philippians 2:9. And his name shall be called Wonderful Counselor, The Mighty God, The Everlasting Father, the Prince of Peace. Isaiah 9:6.

76   I Will Bring the Blind
Isaiah 42:16

I Will Call Upon God
Psalm 55:16,17

77

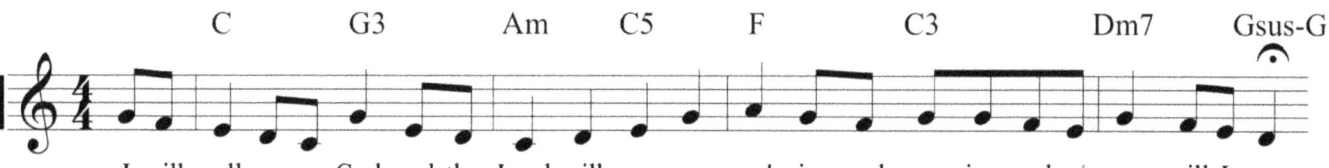

I Will Come to You
John 14:18,20

78

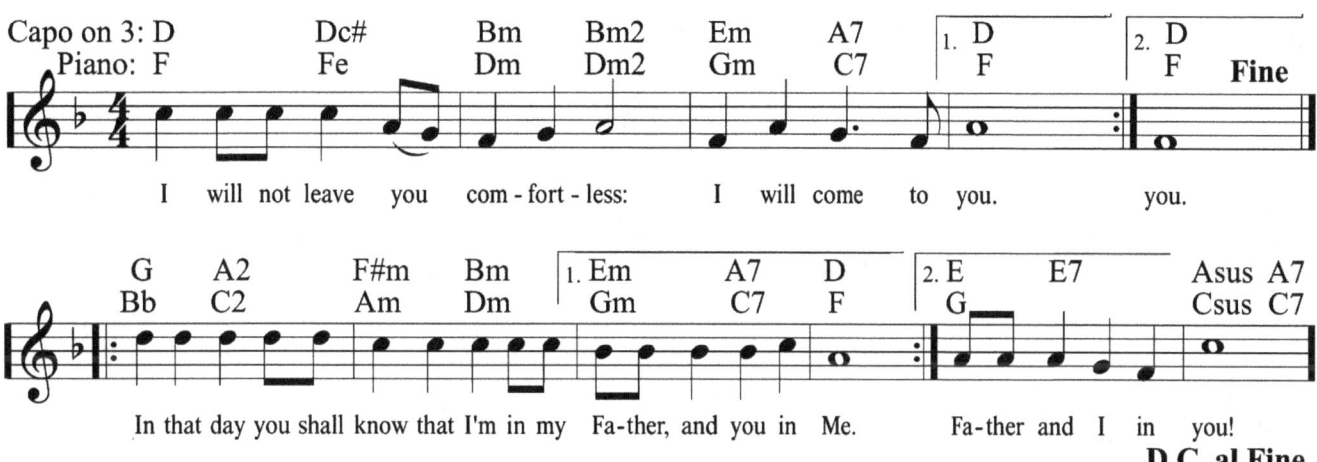

That Christ may dwell in your hearts by faith. Ephesians 3:17. Let the word of Christ dwell in you richly in all wisdom. Colossians 3:16. Ye are not in the flesh, but in the Spirit, if so be that the Spirit of God dwell in you. Now if any man have not the Spirit of Christ, he is none of His. And if Christ be in you…the Spirit is life. Romans 8:9,10. Now the Lord is that Spirit. 2Corinthians 3:17. The last Adam was made a quickening spirit. 1Corinthians 15:45. The prophets have inquired and searched diligently, who prophesied…searching what, or what manner of time the Spirit of Christ which was in them did signify, when it testified beforehand the sufferings of Christ. 1Peter 1:10,11. For the testimony of Jesus is the spirit of prophecy. Revelation 19:10.

79 I Will Give Them a Heart
Jeremiah 24:7

80 I Will Lift Up Mine Eyes
Psalm 121:1,2

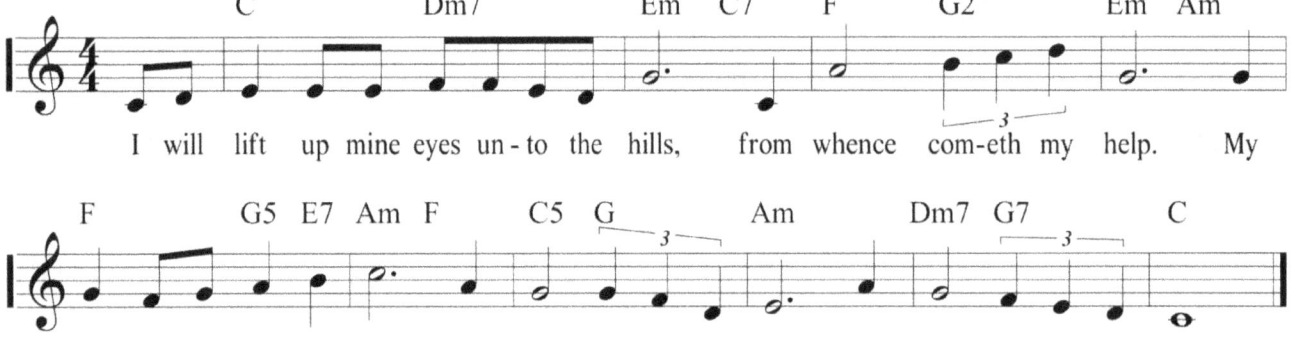

To whom then will ye liken me, or shall I be equal? saith the Holy One. Lift up your eyes on high, and behold who hath created these things, that bringeth out their hosts by number: He calleth them all by names by the greatness of His might, for that He is strong in power; not one faileth…Hast thou not known? Hast thou not heard, that the everlasting God, the LORD, the Creator of the ends of the earth, fainteth not, neither is weary? There is no searching of His understanding. Isaiah 40:25,26,28.

I Will Pour Water 81
Isaiah 44:3,4

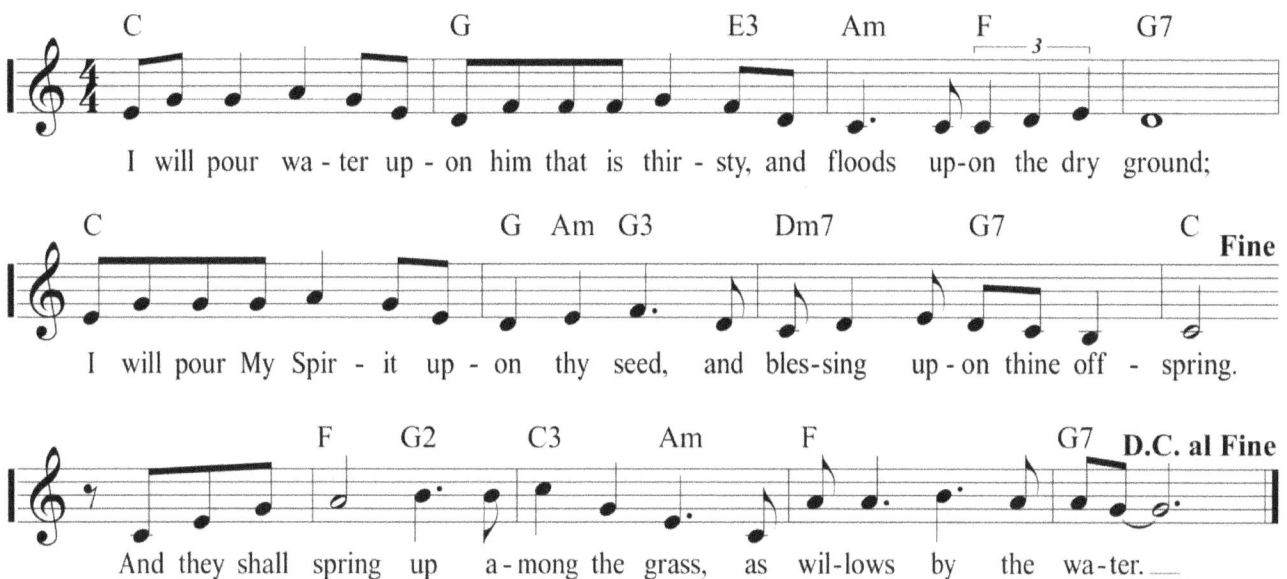

I Will Praise Thee 82
Psalm 86:12

Make a joyful noise unto the LORD, all ye lands. Serve the LORD with gladness: come before His presence with singing. Know ye that the LORD He is God: it is He that hath made us, and not we ourselves; we are His people, and the sheep of His pasture. Enter into His gates with thanksgiving, and into His courts with praise: be thankful unto Him, and bless His name. For the LORD is good; His mercy is everlasting; and His truth endureth to all generations. Psalm 100.

83 If a Man Love Me
John 14:23; Romans 8:9-11

84 If Any Man Be in Christ
2 Corinthians 5:17

If Any Man Sin   85
1 John 2:1; 1:9

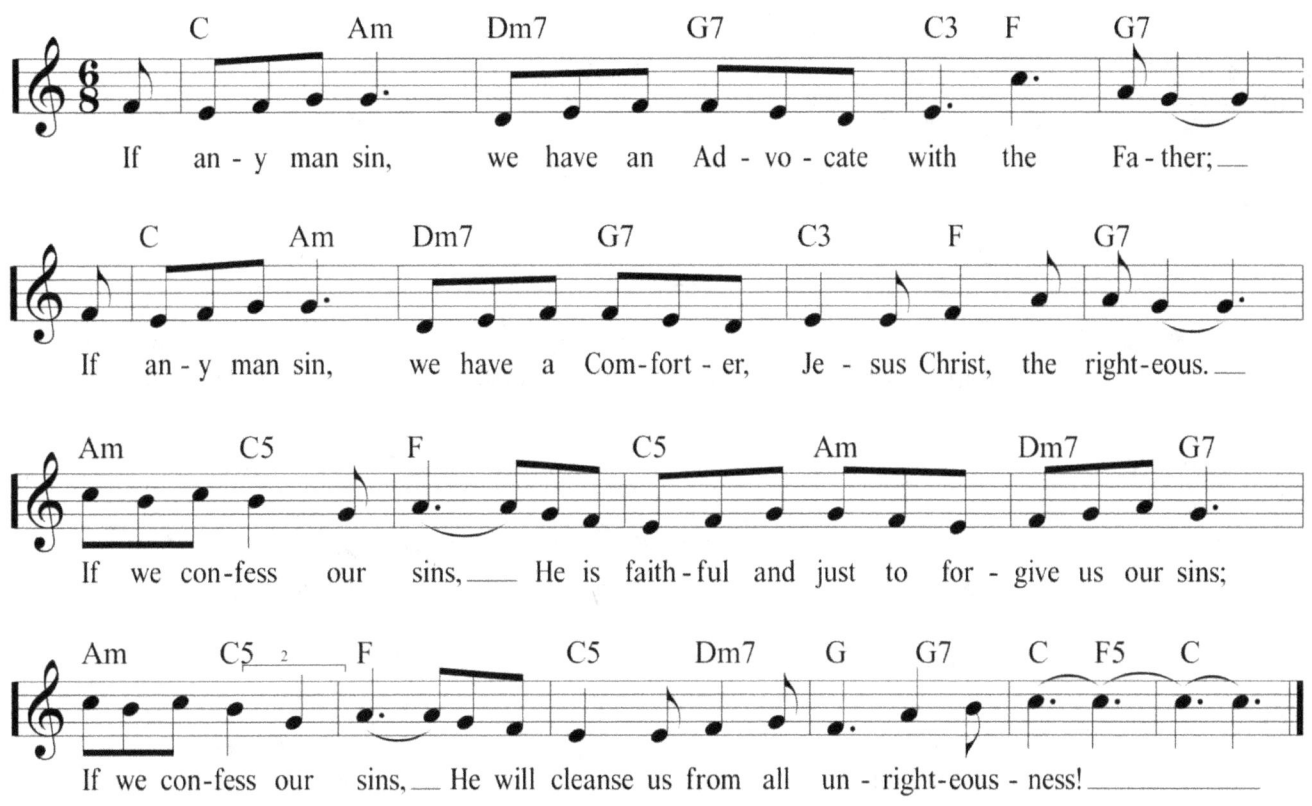

If any man sin, we have an Advocate with the Father;
If any man sin, we have a Comforter, Jesus Christ, the righteous.
If we confess our sins, He is faithful and just to forgive us our sins;
If we confess our sins, He will cleanse us from all unrighteousness!

Advocate, Comforter, are both translated from the same Greek word: *parakletos*

Who is a God like unto Thee, that pardons iniquity, and passes by the transgression of the remnant of His heritage? He retaineth not His anger forever, because He delights in mercy. He will turn again, He will have compassion upon us; He will subdue our iniquities; and Thou wilt cast all their sins into the depths of the sea. Micah 7:7,8,18,19.

Bless the LORD, O my soul; and all that is within me, bless His holy name.
Bless the LORD, O my soul, and forget not all His benefits:
Who forgiveth all thine iniquities; who healtheth all thy diseases;
Who redeemeth thy life from destruction;
Who crowneth thee with lovingkindness and tender mercies;
Who satisfieth thy mouth with good things;
so that thy youth is renewed like the eagles. Psalm 103:1-5.

As far as the east is from the west, so far hath he removed our transgressions from us. Like as a father pitieth his children, so the LORD pitieth them that fear Him. For He knoweth our frame; He remembers that we are dust. Psalm 103:12-14.

86 If Two of You
Matthew 18:19,20

The king of Israel, even the LORD, is in the midst of thee: thou shalt not see evil any more…The LORD thy God in the midst of thee is mighty; He will save, He will rejoice over thee with joy; He will rest in His love, He will joy over thee with singing.   Zephaniah 3:15,17.

If Thou Wilt Diligently
Exodus 15:26

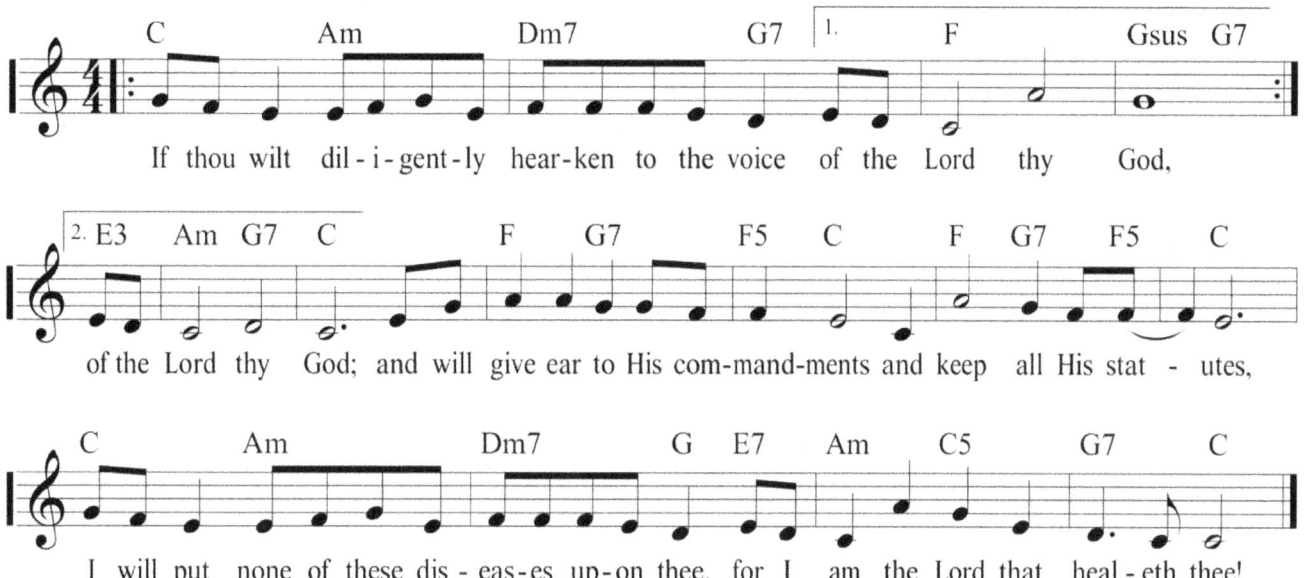

I'm Crucified With Christ
Galatians 2:20; 1Peter 1:3

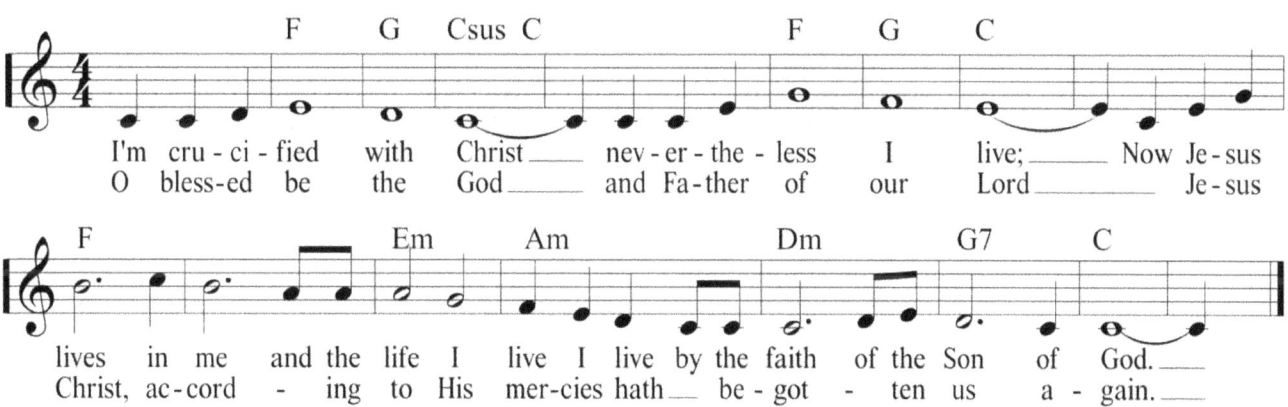

If any man will come after Me, let him deny himself, and take up his cross, and follow Me. For whosoever will save his life shall lose it: and whosoever will lose his life for my sake shall find it. For what is a man profited, if he shall gain the whole world, and lose his own soul? Or what shall a man give in exchange for his soul? Matthew 16:24-26.

God forbid that I should glory, save in the cross of our Lord Jesus Christ, by whom the world is crucified unto me, and I unto the world. Galatians 6:14.

89 In That Day There Shall Be a Fountain
Zechariah 12:10; 13:1

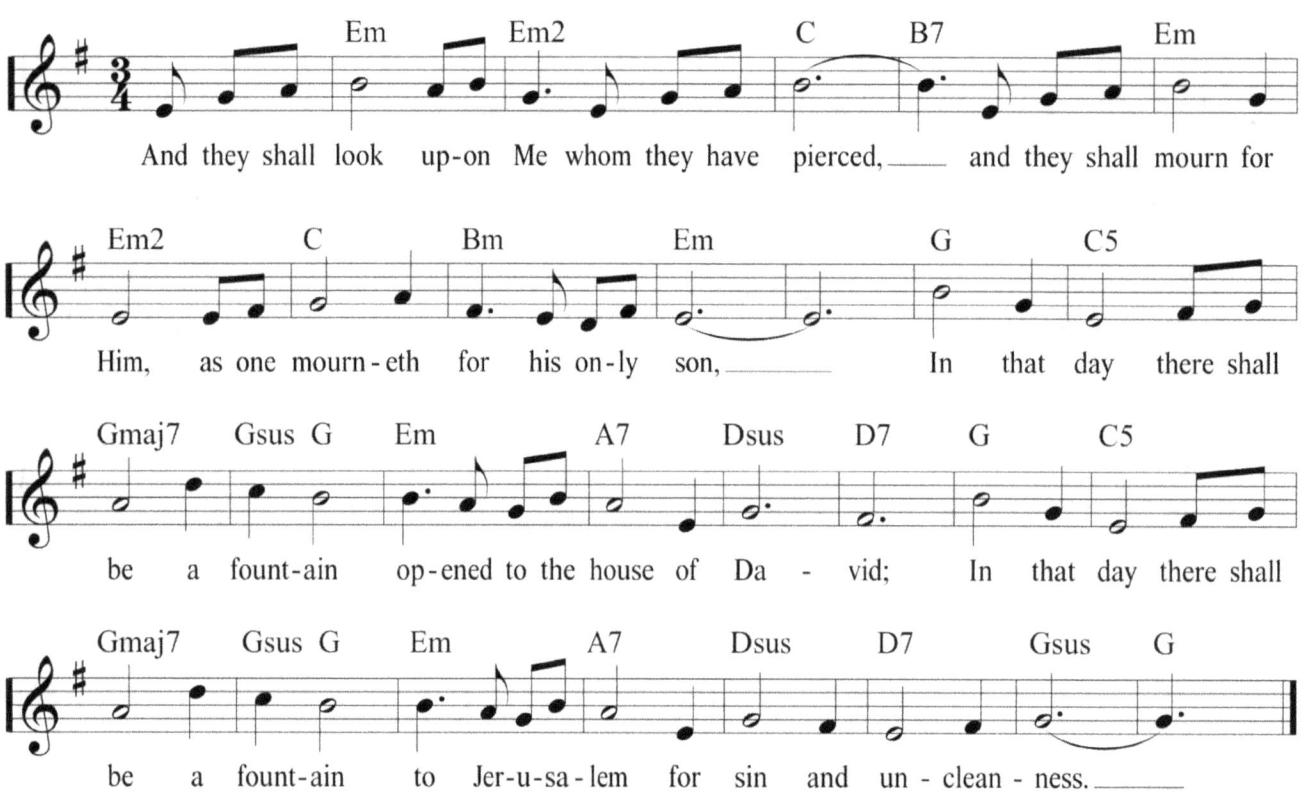

90 In This Was Manifested
1 John 4:9

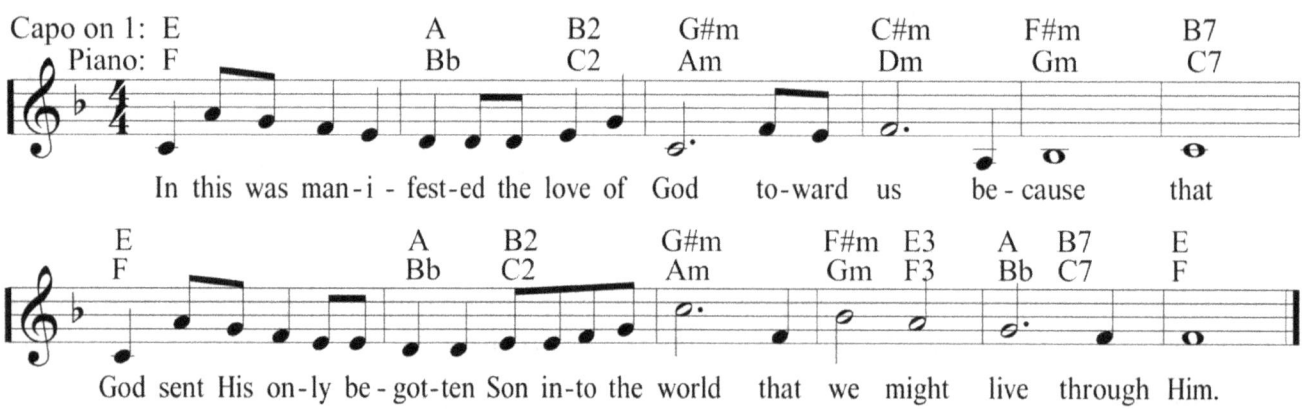

God sent not His Son into the world to condemn the world, but that the world through him might be saved. John 3:17. Thou art the Son of God, which should come into the world. John 11:27. Holy Father...Thou hast sent me into the world. John 17:11,18. He bringeth in the firstbegotten into the world. Hebrews 1:6.

In the Beginning 91
John 1:1; Philippians 2:6,9

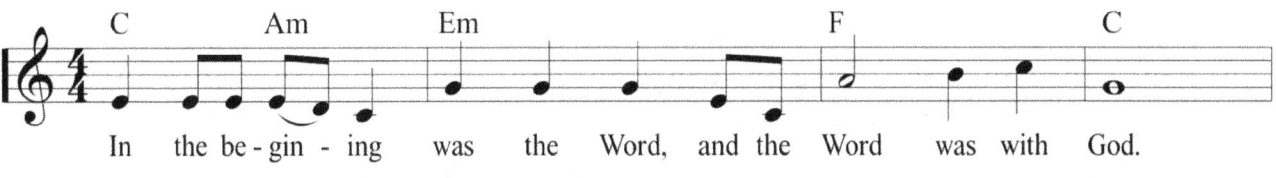
In the be-gin-ing was the Word, and the Word was with God.

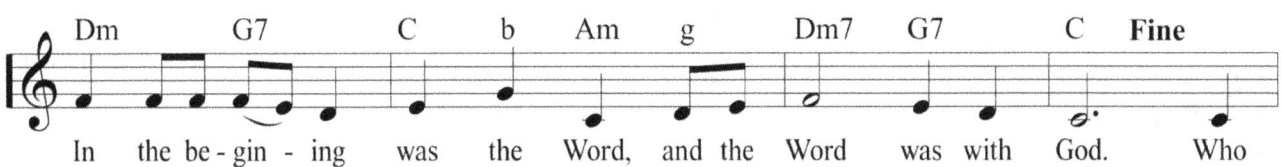
In the be-gin-ing was the Word, and the Word was with God. Who

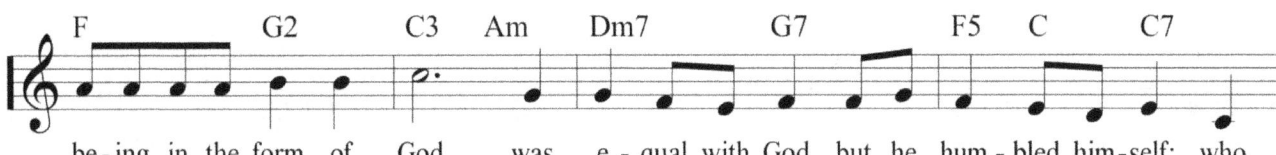
be-ing in the form of God, was e-qual with God but he hum-bled him-self; who

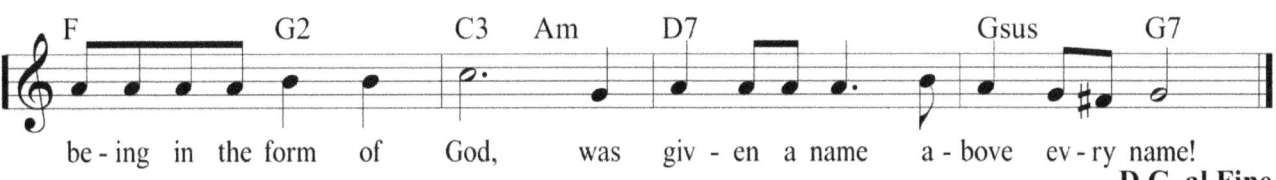
be-ing in the form of God, was giv-en a name a-bove ev-ry name!
D.C. al Fine

Judge Not 92
Luke 6:37,38

Judge not, and ye shall not be judged; con-demn not, and ye shall not be con-demned; For-

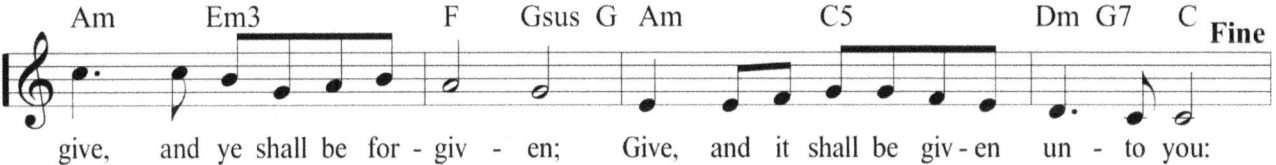
give, and ye shall be for-giv-en; Give, and it shall be giv-en un-to you:

Good mea-sure, pressed down, and shak-en to-geth-er, and run-ning ov-er, run-ning ov-er.
rit. **D.C. al Fine**

93 Labor Not
John 6:27

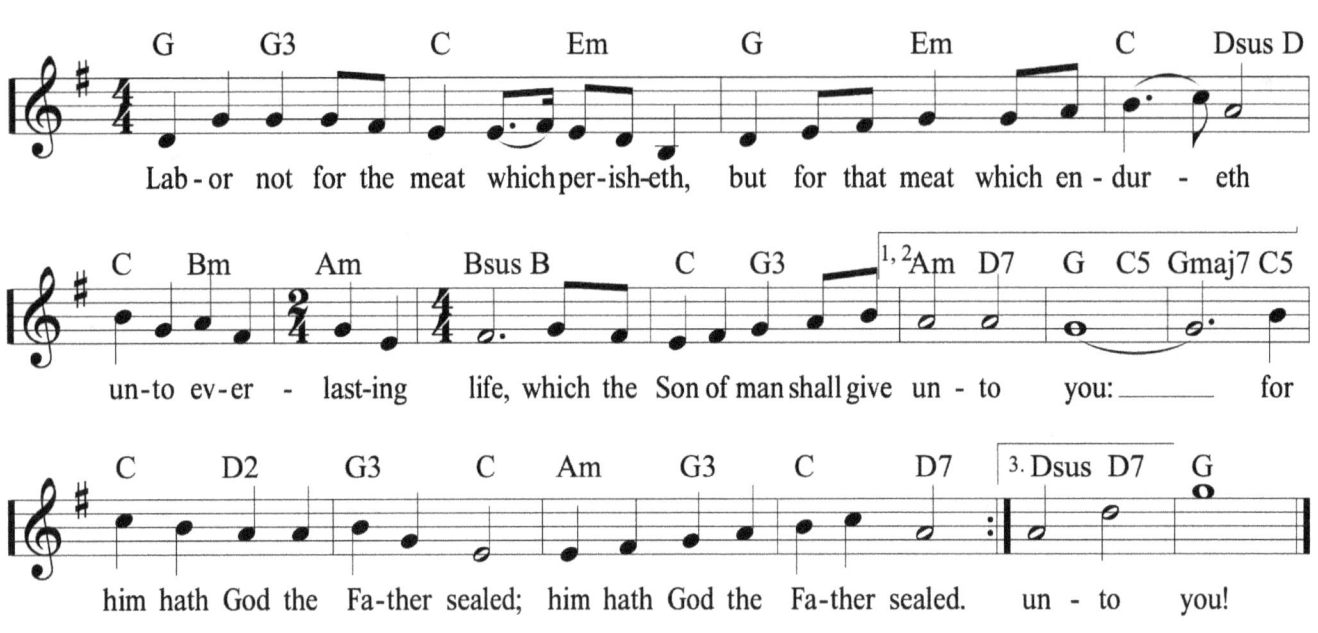

94 Lead Me to the Rock
Psalm 61:1-4

Let Not the Wise Man
Jeremiah 9:23,24

95

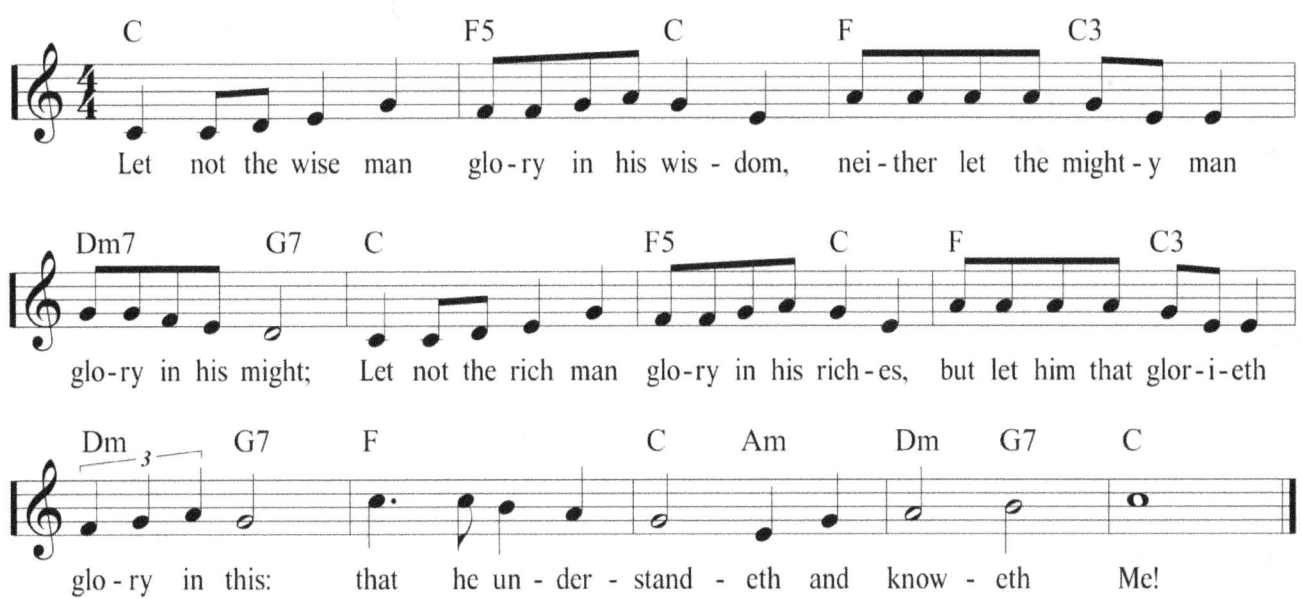

Let the Word of Christ
Colossians 3:16

96

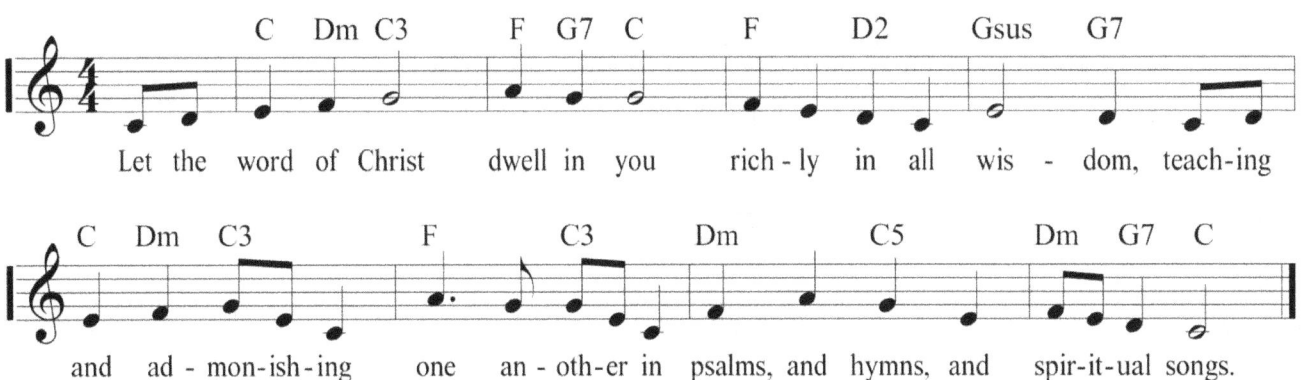

If ye abide in Me, and My words abide in you, ye shall ask what ye will, and it shall be done unto you. John 15:7.

That He would grant you, according to the riches of His glory, to be strengthened with might by His Spirit in the inner man; That Christ may dwell in your hearts by faith. Ephesians 3:16,17.

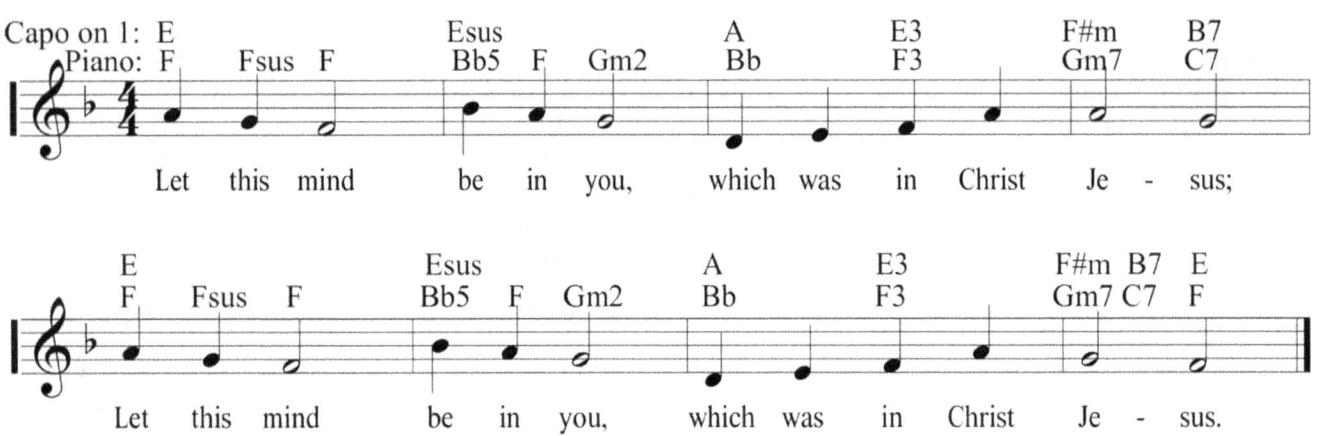

Who, being in the form of God, thought it not robbery to be equal with God: But made himself of no reputation, and took upon him the form of a servant, and was made in the likeness of men. Philippians 2:6,7,

Fulfil ye my joy, that ye be likeminded, having the same love, being of one accord, of one mind. Let nothing be done through strife or vainglory; but in lowliness of mind let each esteem other better than themselves. Philippians 2:2,3.

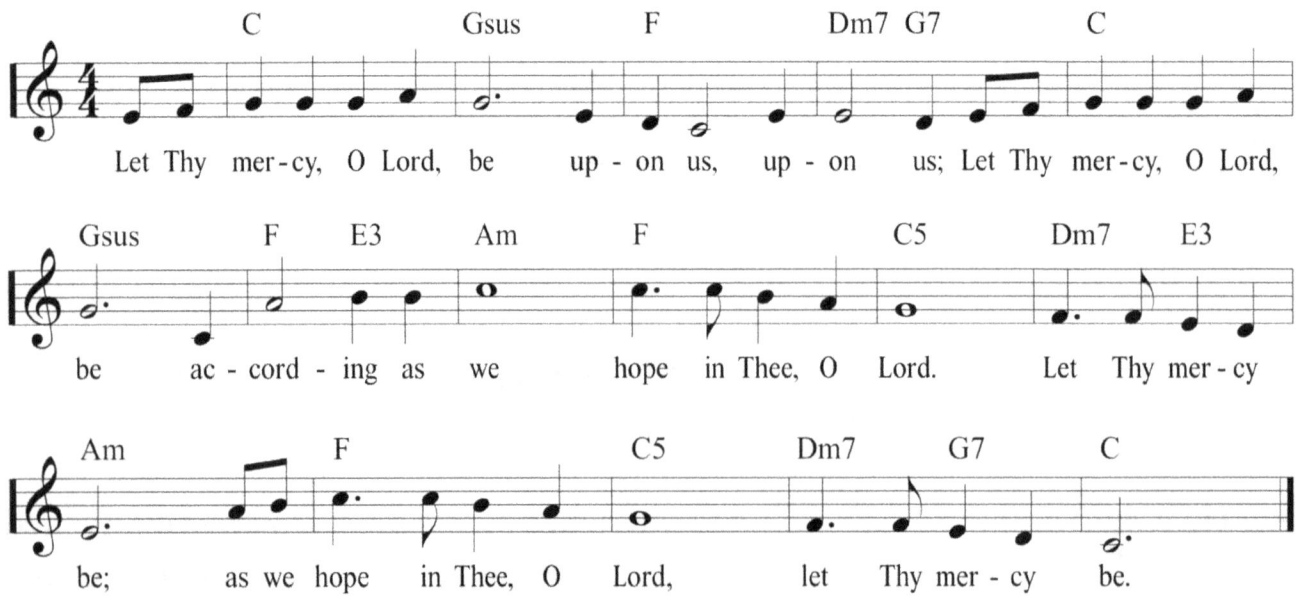

Let Us Hold Fast 99

Hebrews 10:23,24

Lift up Your Eyes on High 100

Isaiah 40:26

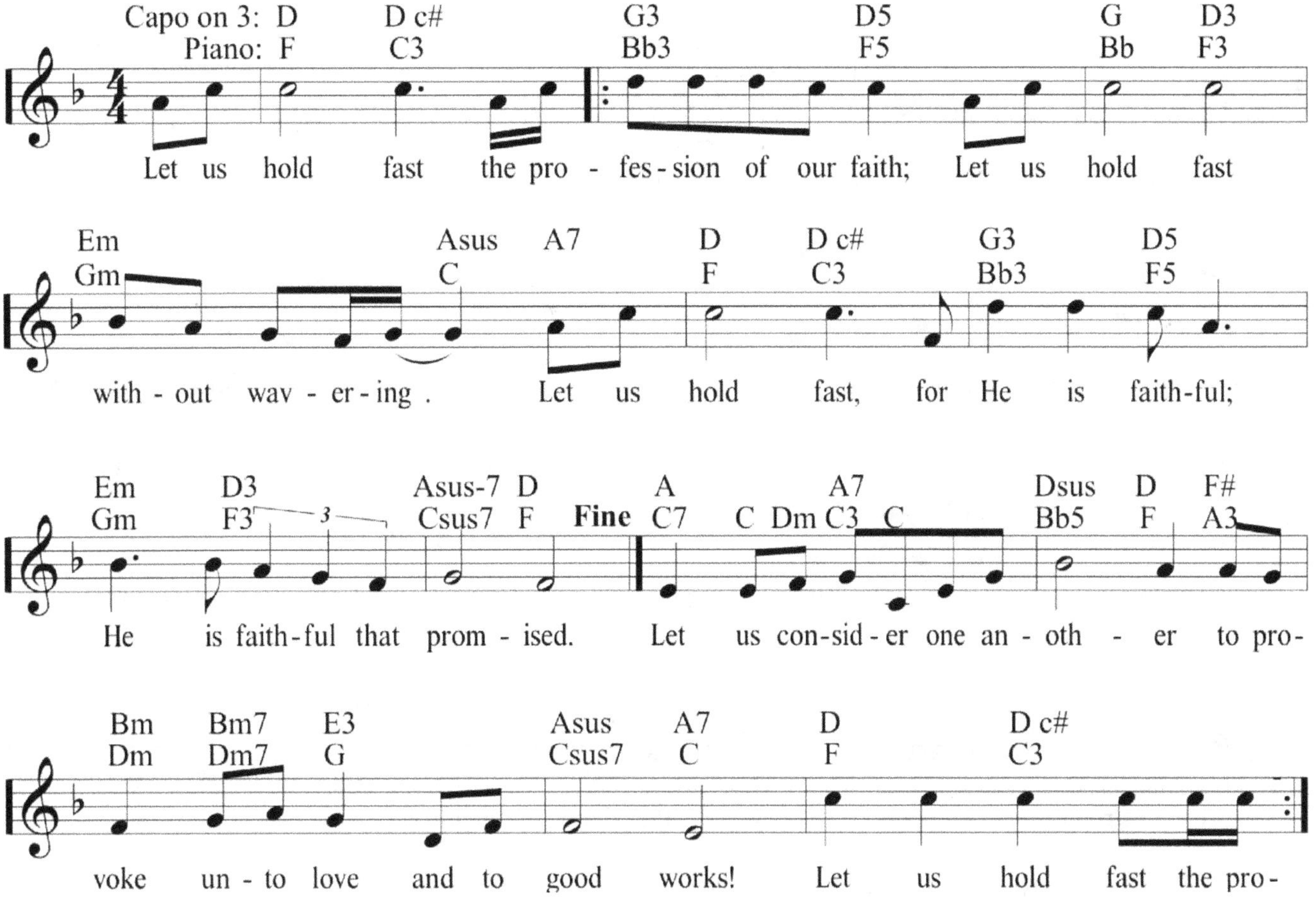

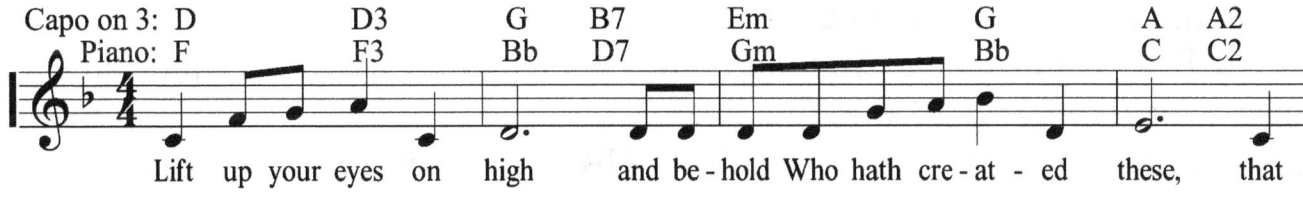

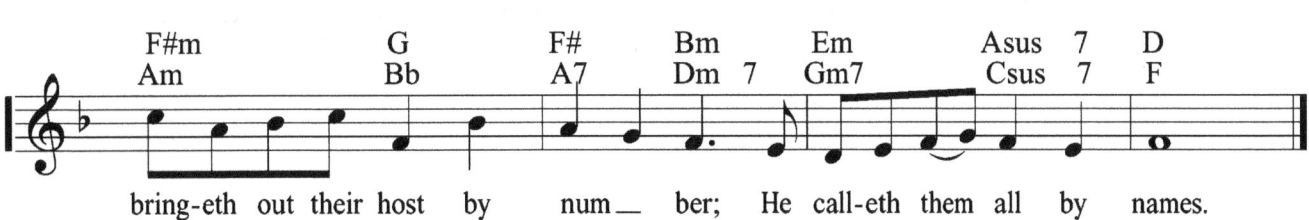

101   Lift up Your Head O Ye Gates
Psalm 24:7-10

And I saw heaven opened, and behold a white horse; and He that sat upon him was called Faithful and True…His eyes were as a flame of fire, and on his head were many crowns; and he had a name written, that no man knew, but He Himself. And He was clothed with a vesture dipped in blood: and His name is called The Word of God. And the armies which were in heaven followed Him upon white horses, clothed in fine linen, white and clean. And out of His mouth goeth a sharp sword…And He hath on His vesture and on His thigh a name written, KING OF KINGS, AND LORD OF LORDS. Revelation 19:11-16.

Living Waters
John 4:10,14

102

103   Lo, I See Four Men
Daniel 3:25

Then Nebuchadnezzar the king was astonished, and rose up in haste, and spake, and said unto his counsellors, Did not we cast three men bound into the midst of the fire? They answered and said, True, O king. He answered and said,

104   Lo, This is Our God
Isaiah 25:9

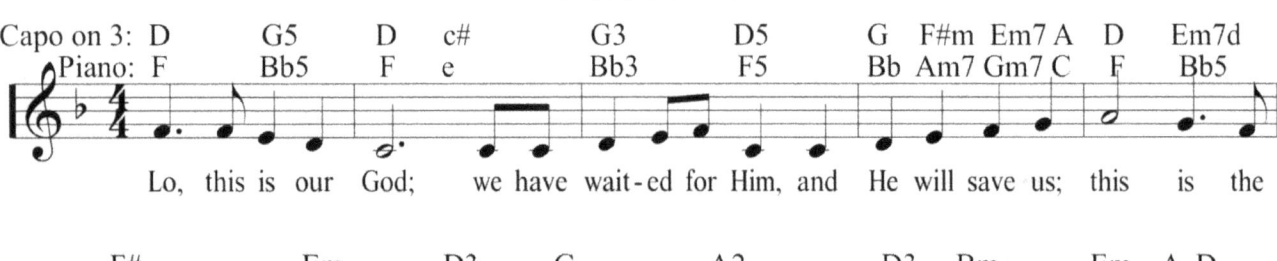

Looking unto Jesus 105

Hebrew 12:1,2

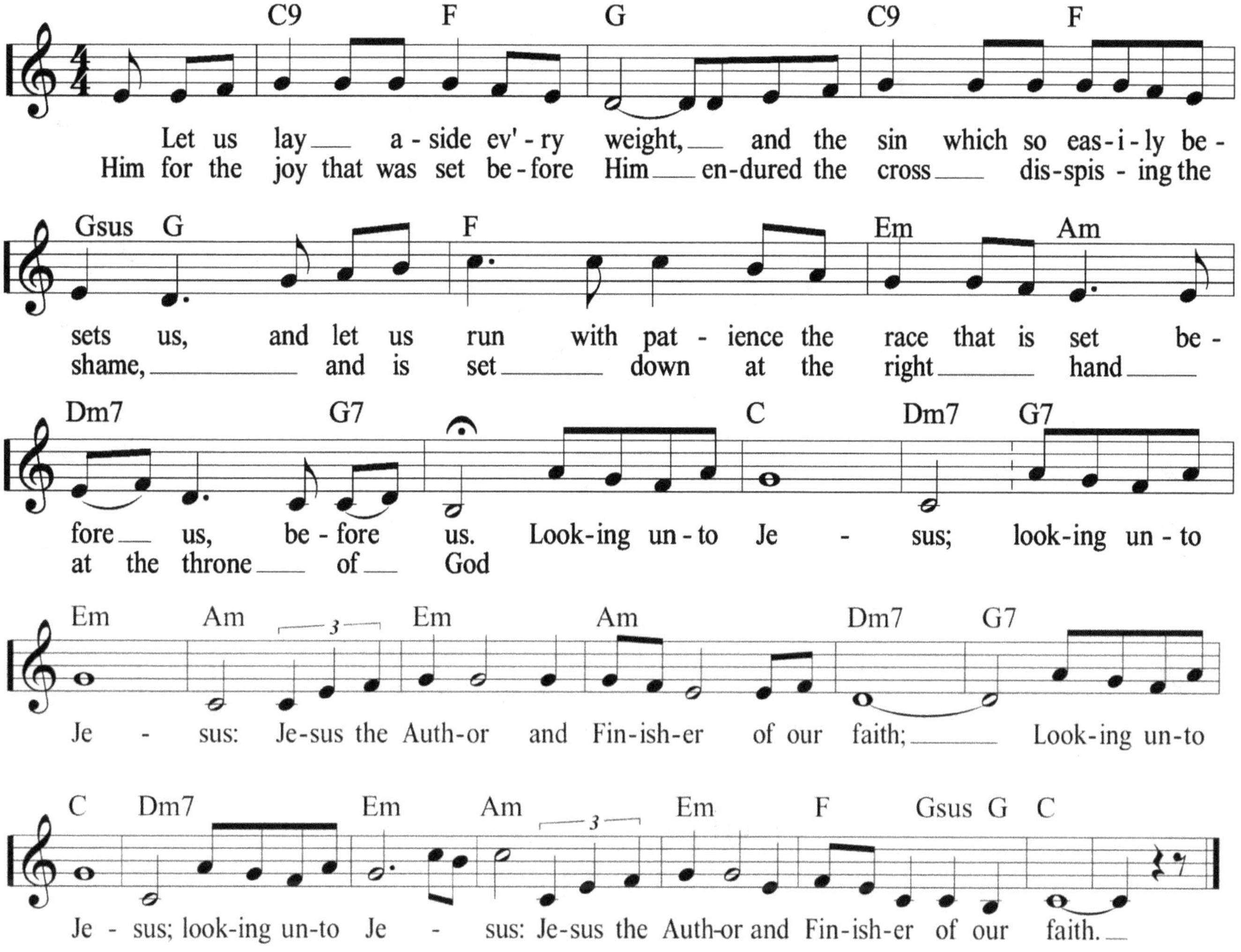
C9 F G C9 F
Let us lay a - side ev' - ry weight, and the sin which so eas-i-ly be -
Him for the joy that was set be-fore Him en-dured the cross dis-spis - ing the
Gsus G F Em Am
sets us, and let us run with pat - ience the race that is set be -
shame, and is set down at the right hand
Dm7 G7 C Dm7 G7
fore us, be - fore us. Look-ing un - to Je - sus; look-ing un - to
at the throne of God
Em Am Em Am Dm7 G7
Je - sus: Je-sus the Auth-or and Fin-ish-er of our faith; Look-ing un-to
C Dm7 Em Am Em F Gsus G C
Je - sus; look-ing un-to Je - sus: Je-sus the Auth-or and Fin-ish-er of our faith.

Lord Bless Thee 106

Numbers 6:24-26

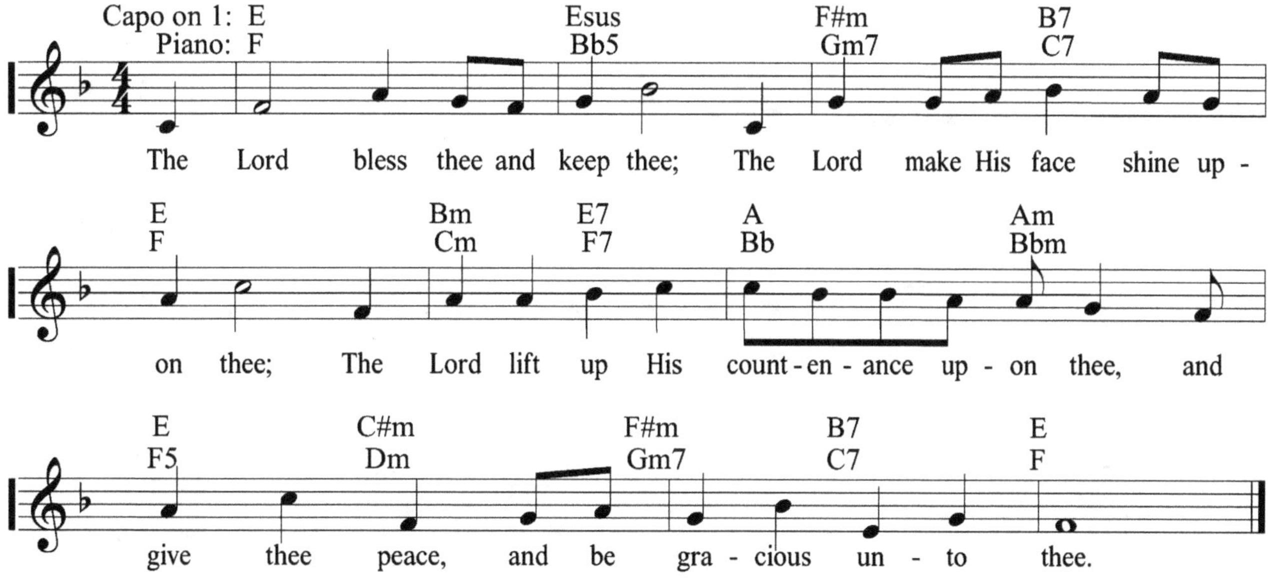
Capo on 1: E Esus F#m B7
Piano: F Bb5 Gm7 C7
The Lord bless thee and keep thee; The Lord make His face shine up -
E Bm E7 A Am
F Cm F7 Bb Bbm
on thee; The Lord lift up His count-en-ance up - on thee, and
E C#m F#m B7 E
F5 Dm Gm7 C7 F
give thee peace, and be gra - cious un - to thee.

107 Lord Himself Shall Descend

1 Thessalonians 4:16,17

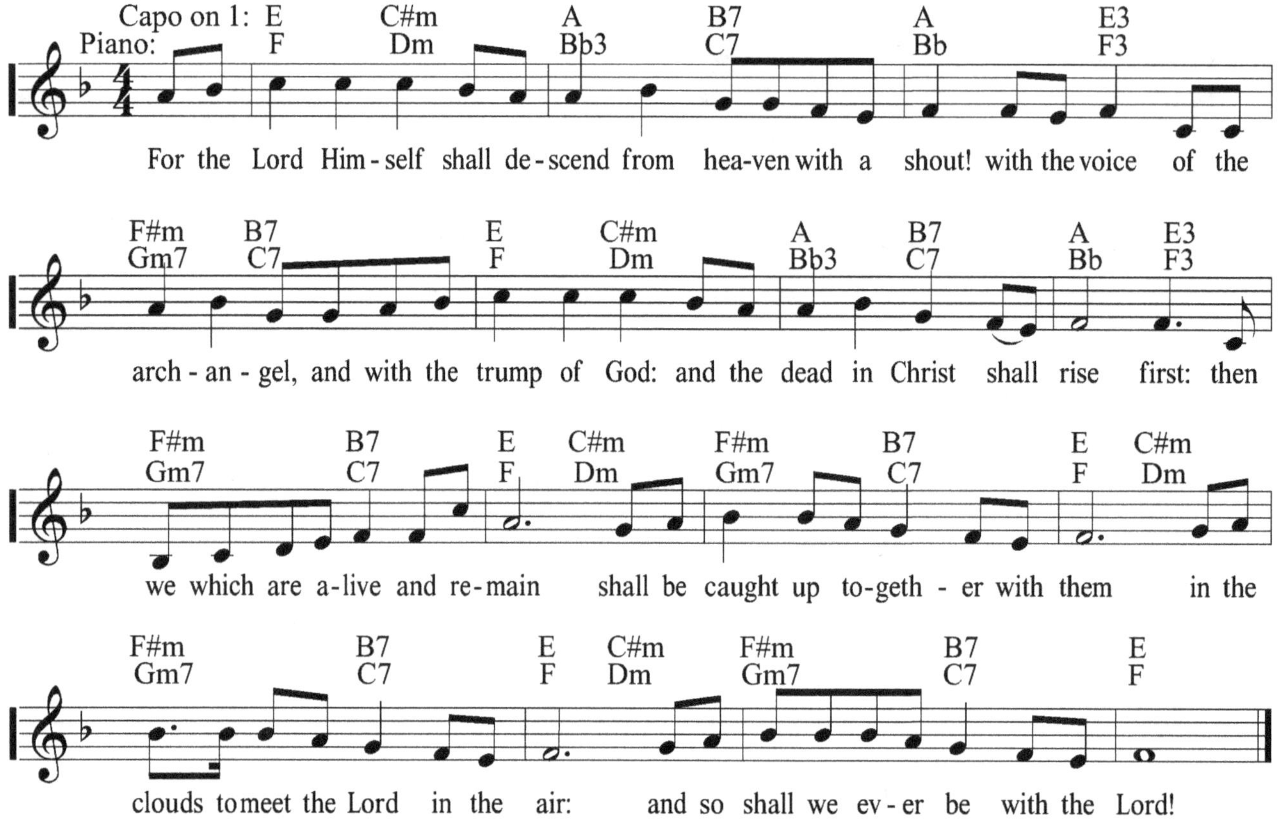
Capo on 1: E C#m A B7 A E3
Piano: F Dm Bb3 C7 Bb F3
For the Lord Him-self shall de-scend from hea-ven with a shout! with the voice of the
F#m B7 E C#m A B7 A E3
Gm7 C7 F Dm Bb3 C7 Bb F3
arch-an-gel, and with the trump of God: and the dead in Christ shall rise first: then
F#m B7 E C#m F#m B7 E C#m
Gm7 C7 F Dm Gm7 C7 F Dm
we which are a-live and re-main shall be caught up to-geth-er with them in the
F#m B7 E C#m F#m B7 E
Gm7 C7 F Dm Gm7 C7 F
clouds to meet the Lord in the air: and so shall we ev-er be with the Lord!

108 Lord, the Lord

Exodus 34:6,7

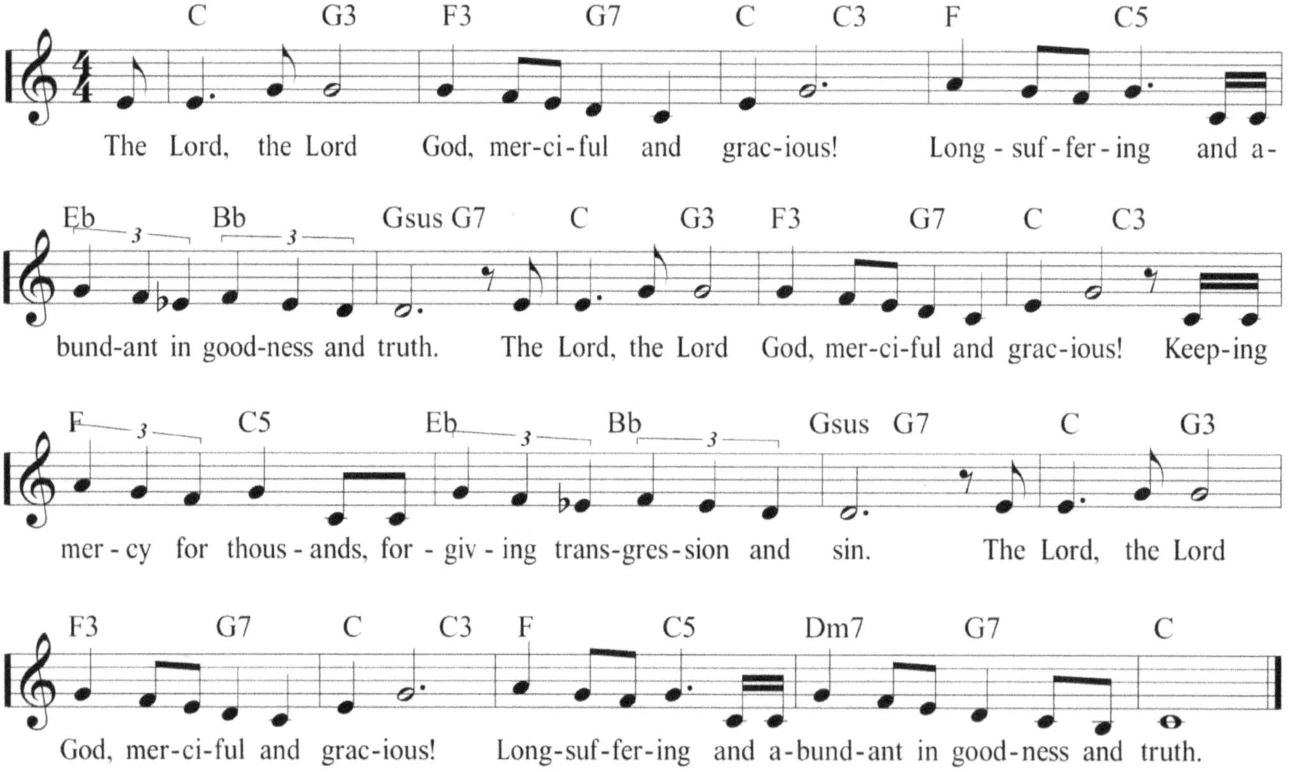
C G3 F3 G7 C C3 F C5
The Lord, the Lord God, mer-ci-ful and grac-ious! Long-suf-fer-ing and a-
Eb Bb Gsus G7 C G3 F3 G7 C C3
bund-ant in good-ness and truth. The Lord, the Lord God, mer-ci-ful and grac-ious! Keep-ing
F C5 Eb Bb Gsus G7 C G3
mer-cy for thous-ands, for-giv-ing trans-gres-sion and sin. The Lord, the Lord
F3 G7 C C3 F C5 Dm7 G7 C
God, mer-ci-ful and grac-ious! Long-suf-fer-ing and a-bund-ant in good-ness and truth.

Lord Possessed Him

109

Proverbs 8:22-24,30

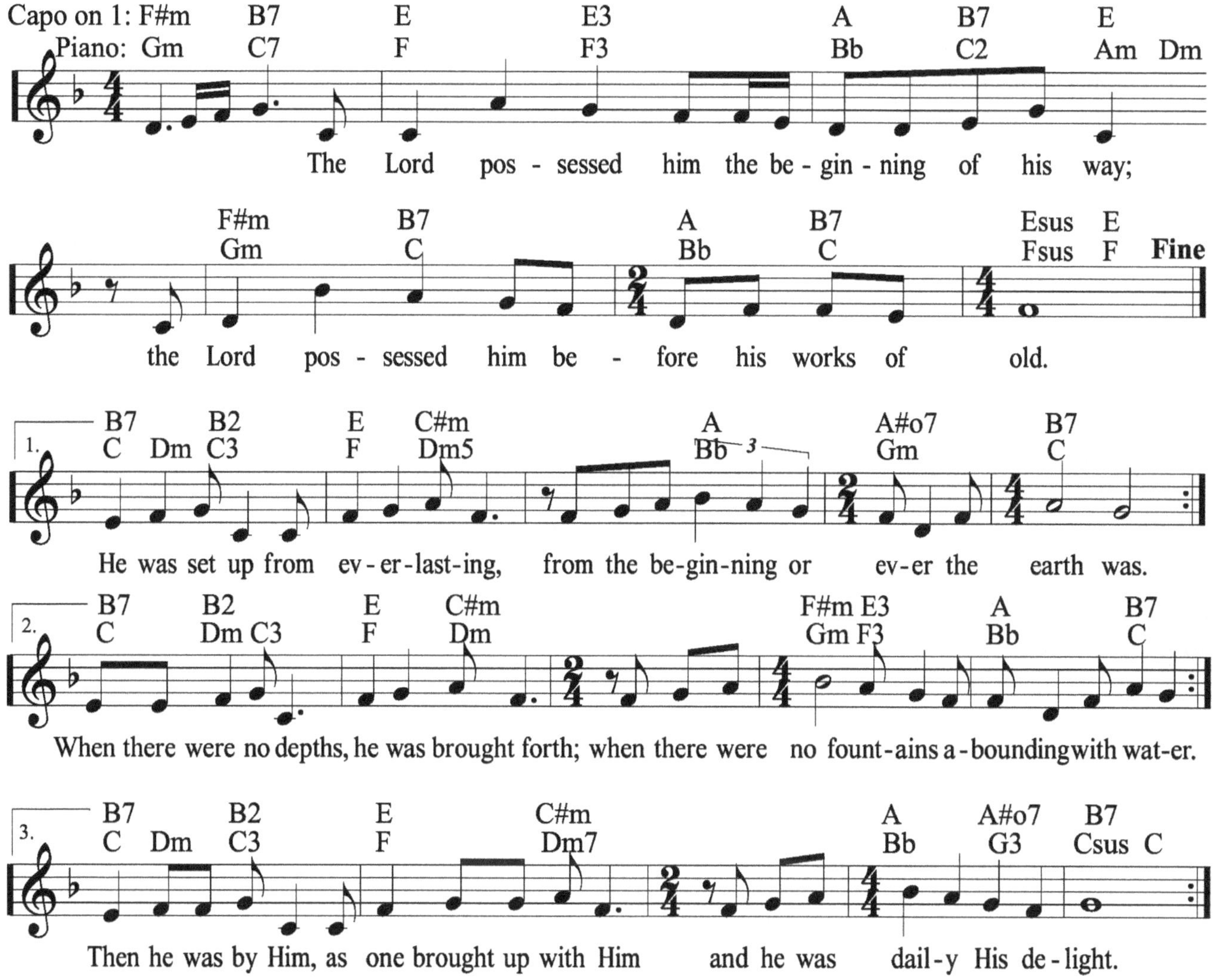
Capo on 1: F#m B7 E E3 A B7 E
Piano: Gm C7 F F3 Bb C2 Am Dm
The Lord pos - sessed him the be - gin - ning of his way;
F#m B7 A B7 Esus E
Gm C Bb C Fsus F Fine
the Lord pos - sessed him be - fore his works of old.
1.
B7 B2 E C#m A A#o7 B7
C Dm C3 F Dm5 Bb Gm C
He was set up from ev - er - last - ing, from the be - gin - ning or ev - er the earth was.
2.
B7 B2 E C#m F#m E3 A B7
C Dm C3 F Dm Gm F3 Bb C
When there were no depths, he was brought forth; when there were no fount - ains a - bounding with wat - er.
3.
B7 B2 E C#m A A#o7 B7
C Dm C3 F Dm7 Bb G3 Csus C
Then he was by Him, as one brought up with Him and he was dail - y His de - light.

Lord Shall Preserve Thee

110

Psalm 121:7,8

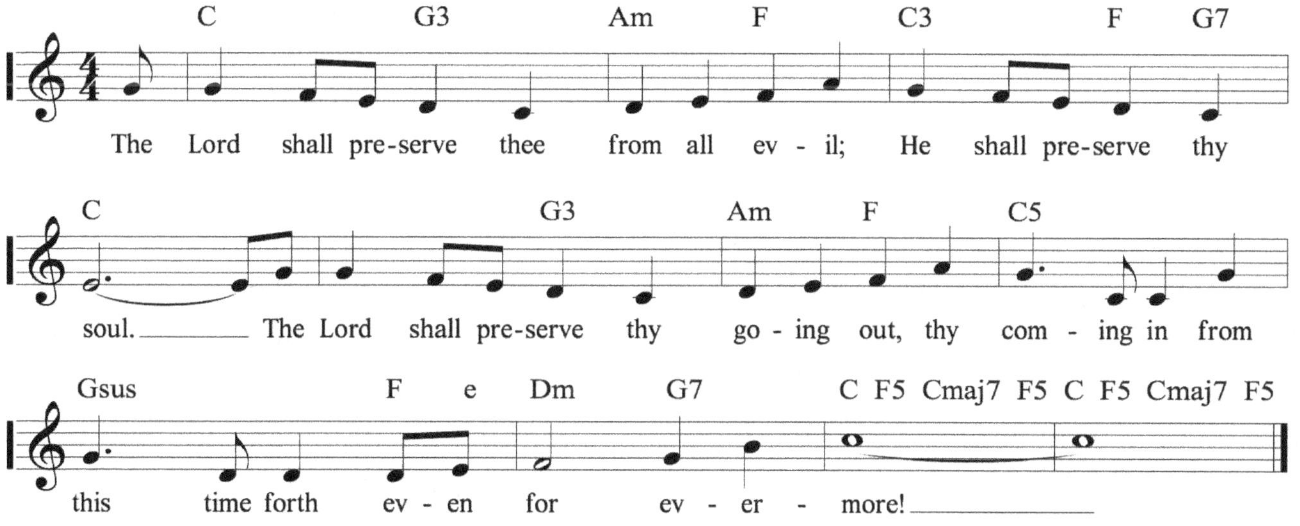
C G3 Am F C3 F G7
The Lord shall pre - serve thee from all ev - il; He shall pre - serve thy
C G3 Am F C5
soul. The Lord shall pre - serve thy go - ing out, thy com - ing in from
Gsus F e Dm G7 C F5 Cmaj7 F5 C F5 Cmaj7 F5
this time forth ev - en for ev - er - more!

111   Lord Thou Hast Been
Psalm 90:1,2

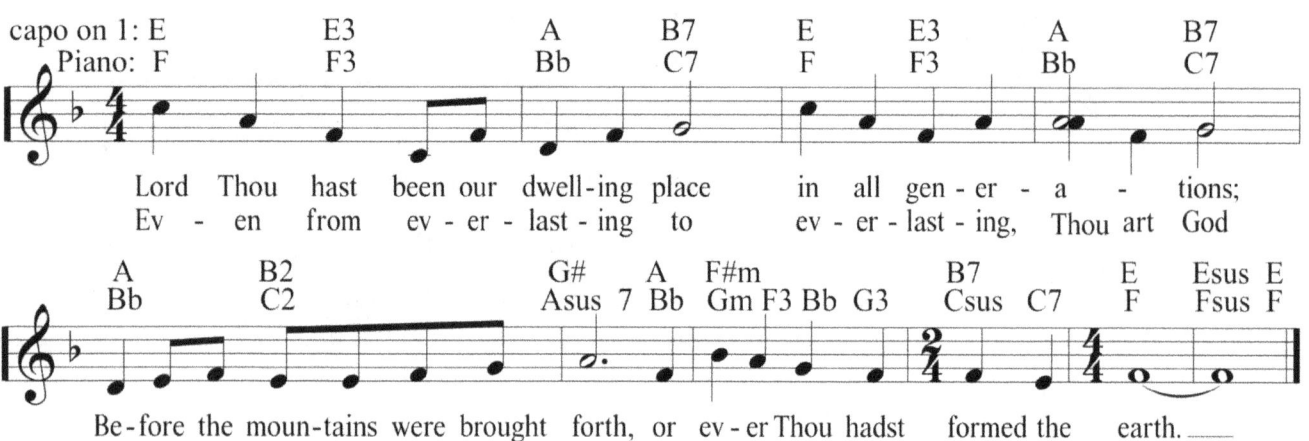

The LORD possessed me [in] the beginning of His way, before His works of old. I was set up from everlasting, from the beginning, or ever the earth was. When there were no depths, I was brought forth; when there were no fountains abounding with water. Before the mountains were settled, before the hills was I brought forth. Proverbs 8:22-25.

112   Love Your Enemies
Matthew 5:44,45

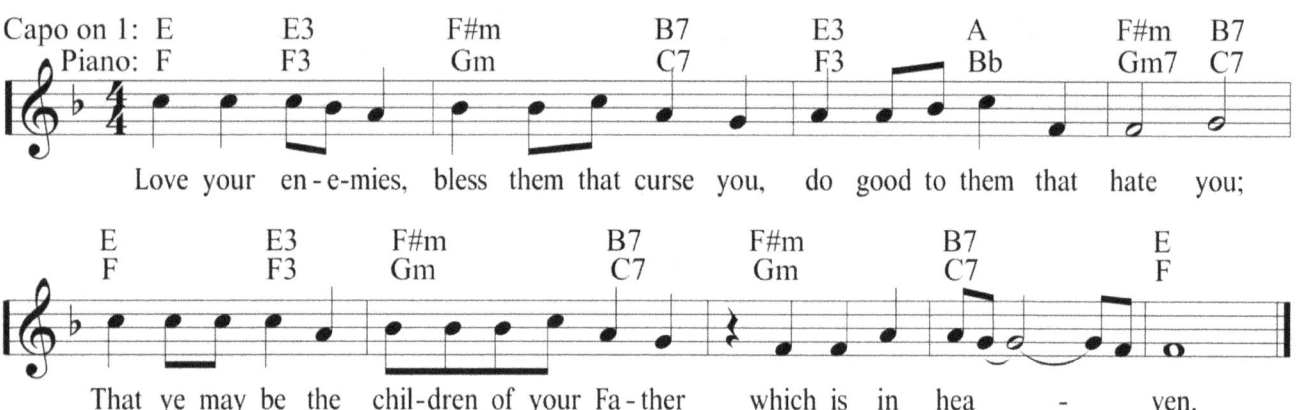

Ye have heard that it hath been said, An eye for an eye, and a tooth for a tooth: But I say unto you, That ye resist not evil: but whosoever shall smite thee on thy right cheek, turn to him the other also. And if any man will sue thee at the law, and take away thy coat, let him have thy cloak also. And whosoever shall compel thee to go a mile, go with him twain. Give to him that asketh thee, and from him that would borrow of thee turn not thou away. Matthew 5:38-42.

Mighty God 113
Psalm 50:1-5

The might-y God, the Lord, hath spo-ken, and called the earth from the ris-ing of the sun.

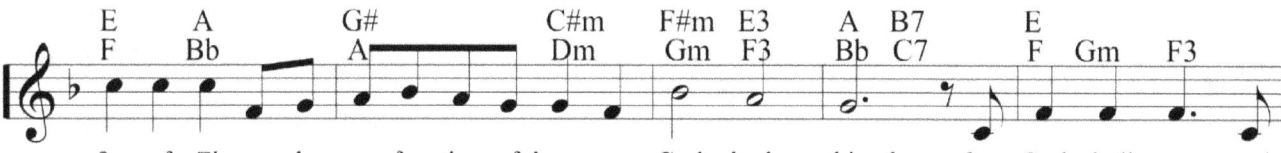
Out of Zi-on, the per-fec-tion of beau-ty, God hath shined. Our God shall come, and

shall not keep si-lence: a fire shall de-vour be-fore Him. He shall call to the

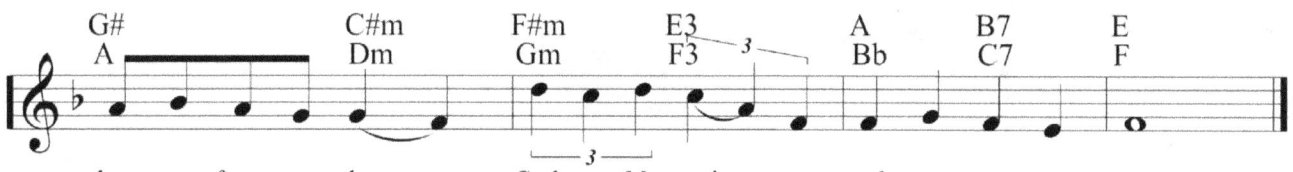
hea-vens from a-bove, Gath-er My saints to-geth-er un-to Me.

Neither is There Salvation 114
Acts 4:12

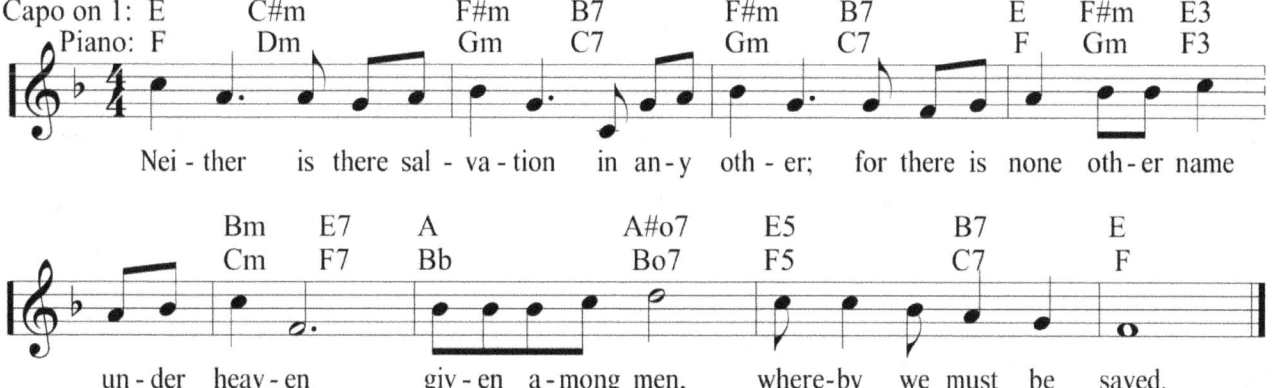
Nei-ther is there sal-va-tion in an-y oth-er; for there is none oth-er name un-der heav-en giv-en a-mong men, where-by we must be saved.

115   No Condemnation
Romans 8:1,2

116   No Fear in Love
1 John 4:18

O Give Thanks unto the Lord 117
Psalm 107:1,2,8

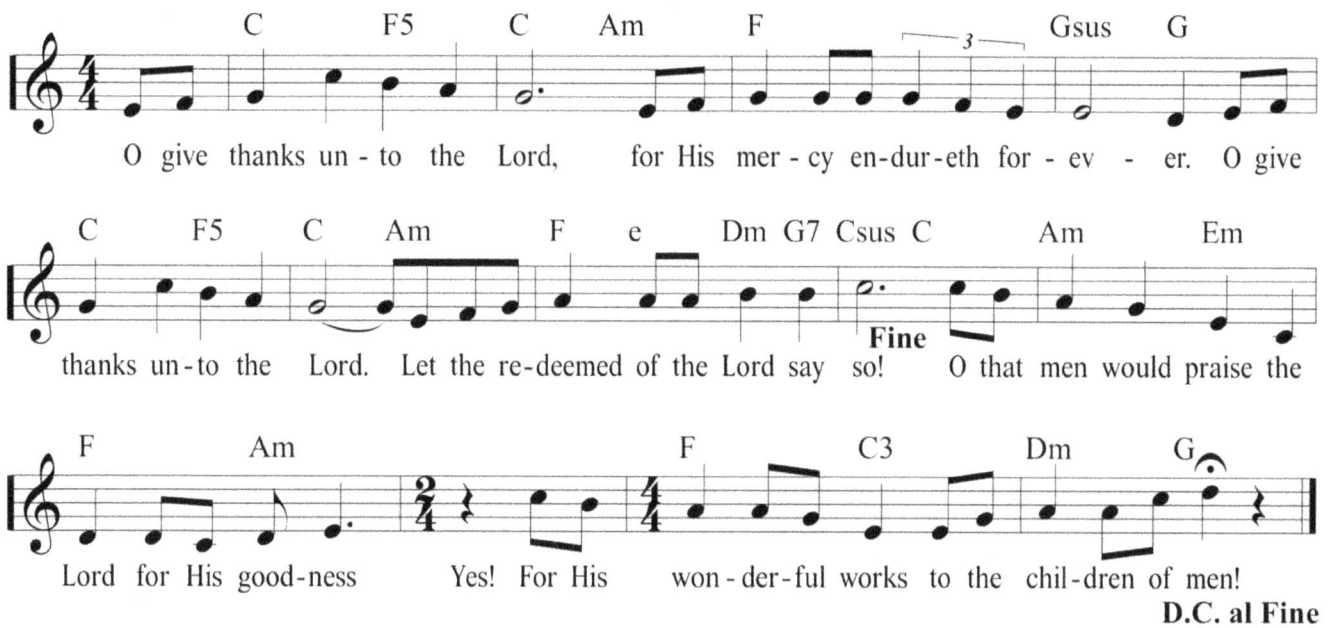

O the Depth of the Riches 118
Romans 11:33

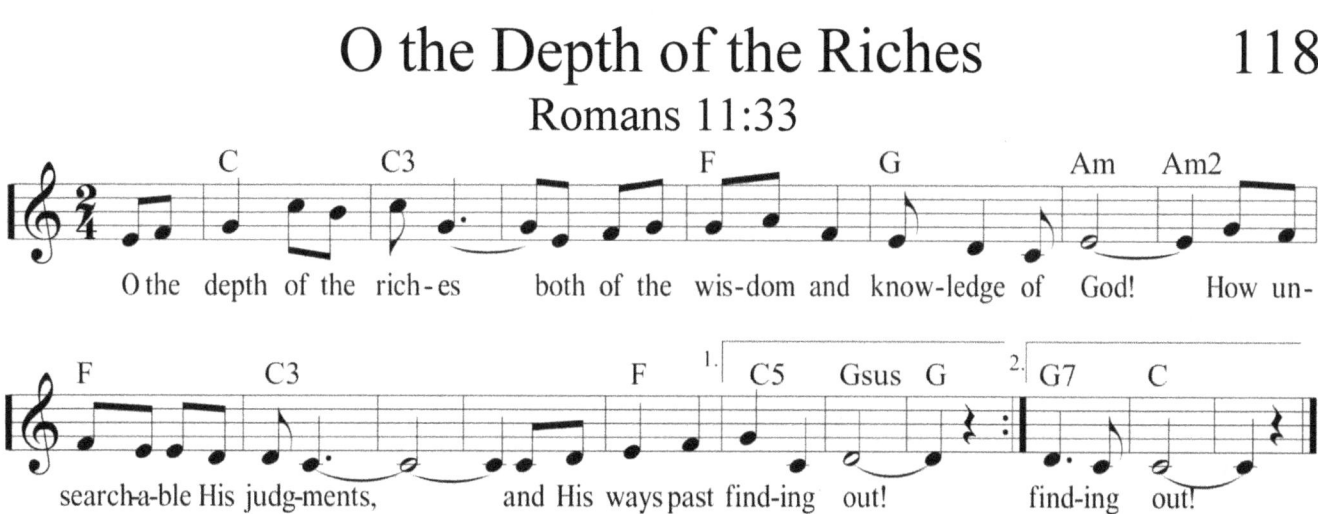

Being knit together in love, and unto all riches of the full assurance of understanding, to the acknowledgment of the mystery of God, and of the Father, and of Christ; in whom are hid all the treasures of wisdom and knowledge. Colossians 2:2,3. Even so, Lord God Almighty, true and righteous are thy judgments. Revelation 16:7.

119 Order My Steps
Psalm 119:133

120 Our Feet Shall Stand
Psalm 122:1,2

Our Light Affliction 121
2 Corinthians 4:17

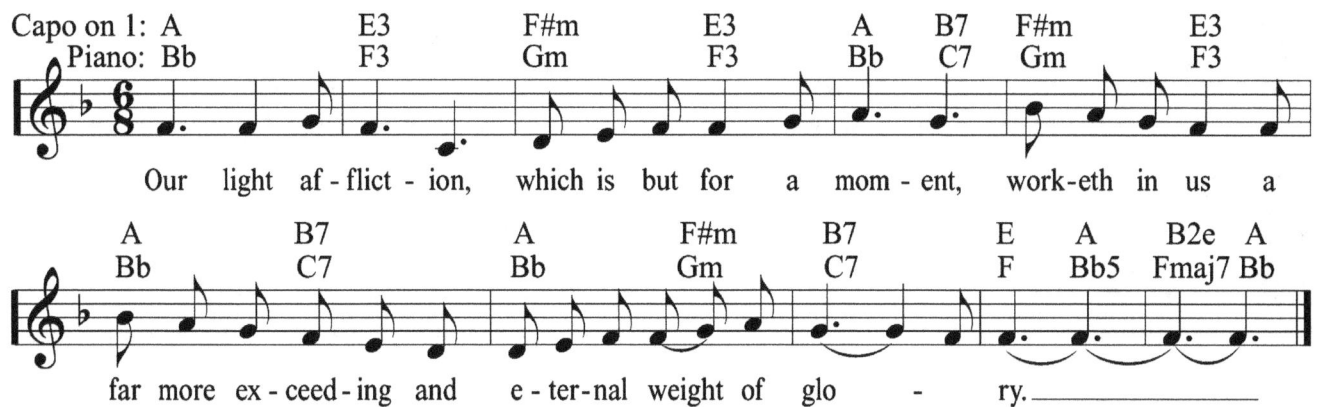

Perfect Peace 122
Isaiah 26:3,4

The meek shall inherit the earth; and shall delight themselves in the abundance of peace. Psalm 37:11 Great peace have they which love Thy law and nothing shall offend them. Psalm 119:165.

123 Precept upon Precept

Isaiah 28:9-11

124 Prophecy Came Not in Old Time

2Peter 1:21; 1Peter 1:11

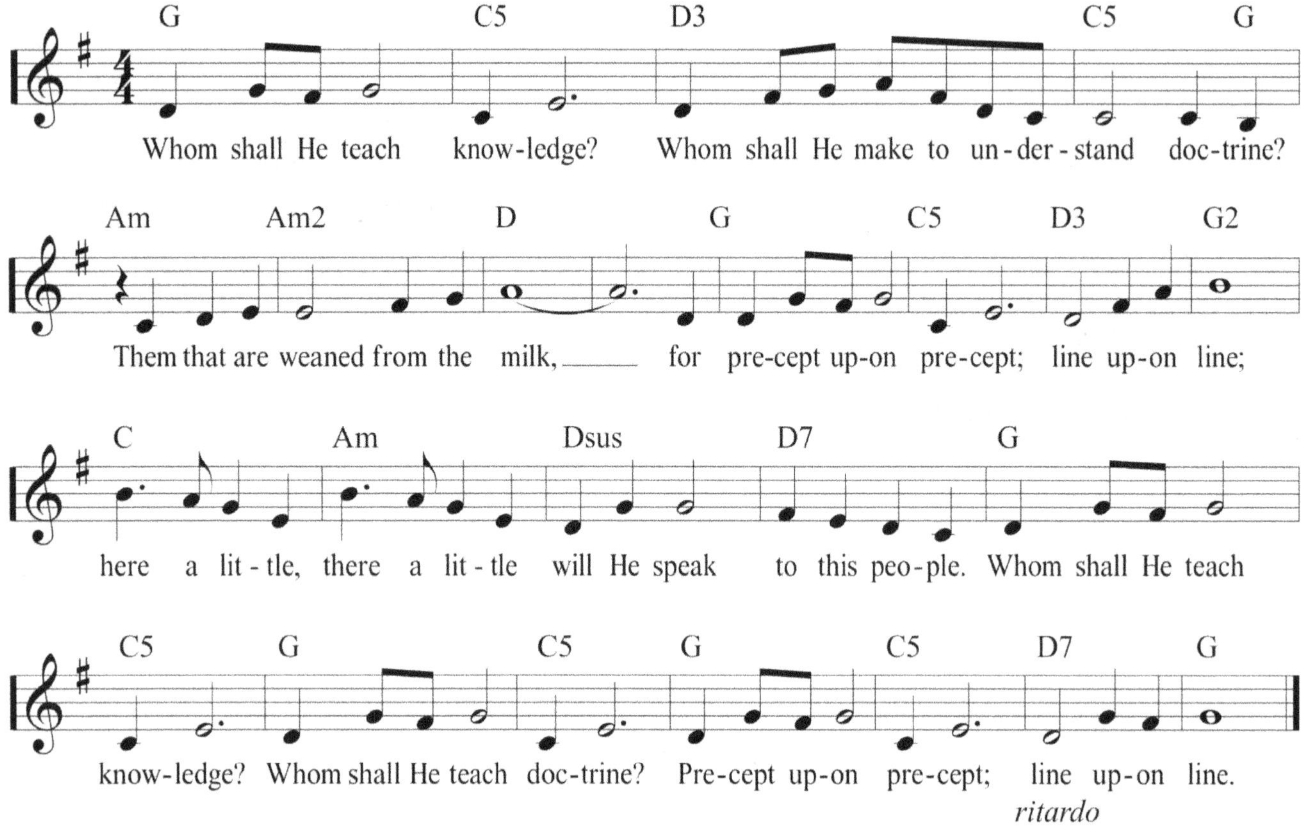

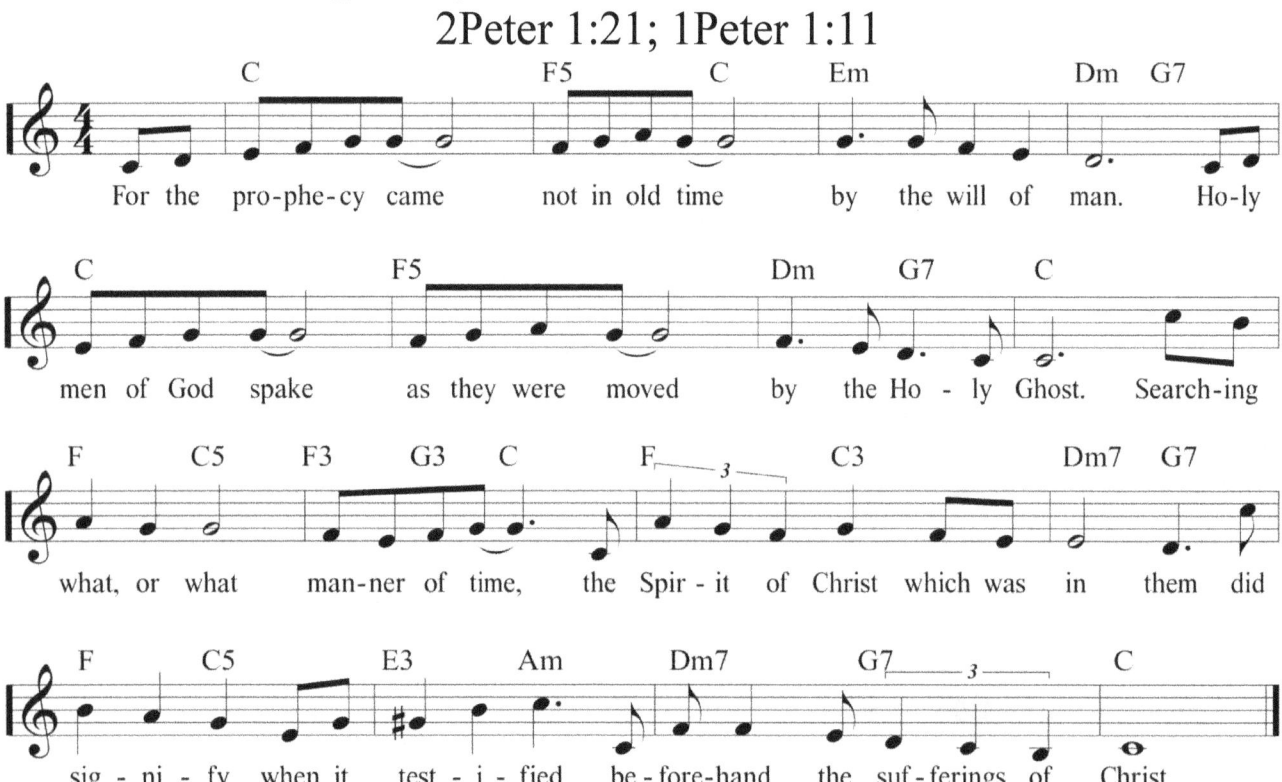

Purge Me with Hyssop
Psalm 51:7,9-11

125

He is faithful and just...to cleanse us from all unrighteousness. 1John 1:9

Raise Up the Foundations
Isaiah 58:12

126

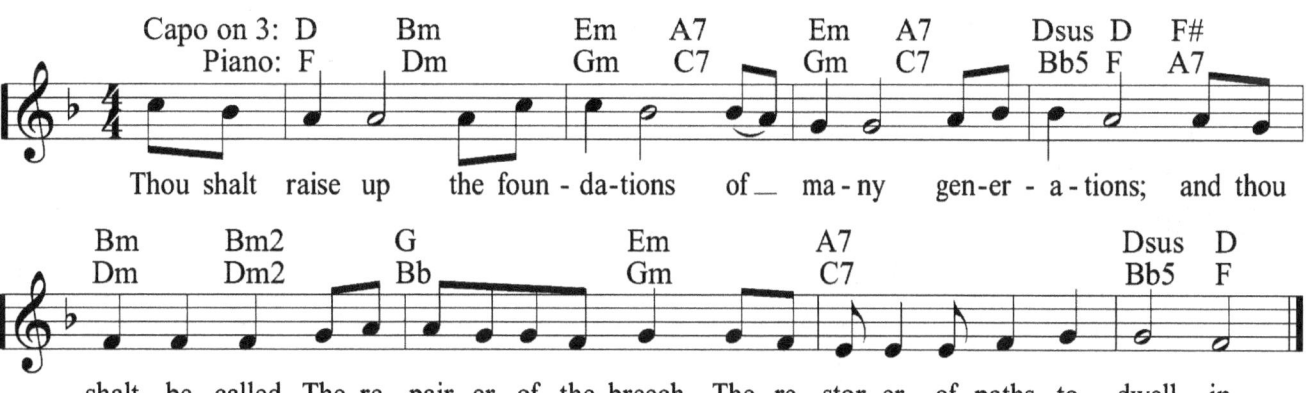

127 Rejoice Evermore
1 Thessalonians 5:16-18

128 Repent, Repent
Acts 2:38

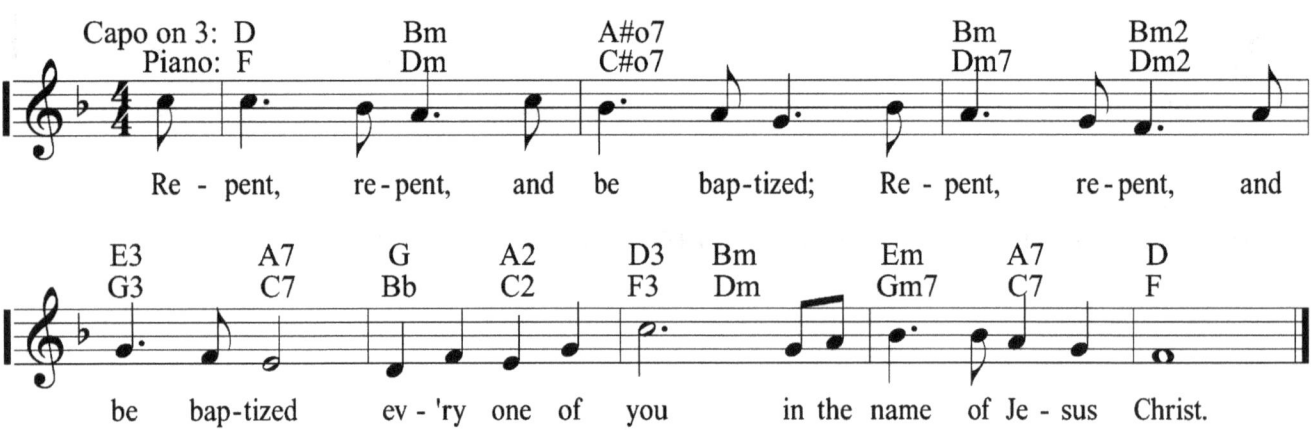

Jesus came into Galilee, preaching the gospel of the kingdom of God, And saying, The time is fulfilled, and the kingdom of God is at hand: repent ye, and believe the gospel. Mark 1:14,15. They that are whole have no need of the physician, but they that are sick: I came not to call the righteous, but sinners to repentance. Mark 2:17. Likewise joy shall be in heaven over one sinner that repenteth, more than over ninety and nine just persons, which need no repentance. Luke 15:7. The goodness of God leadeth thee to repentance. Romans 2:4. Repent, and turn yourselves from all your transgressions; so iniquity shall not be your ruin. Ezekiel 18:30 .

Remember the Sabbath Day 129
Exodus 20:8-11

Concerning the feasts of the LORD, which ye shall proclaim to be holy convocations, even these are my feasts. Six days shall work be done: but the seventh day is the sabbath of rest, an holy convocation; ye shall do no work therein: it is the sabbath of the LORD in all your dwellings. Leviticus 23:2,3. Verily my sabbaths ye shall keep: for it is a sign between me and you throughout your generations; that ye may know that I am the LORD that doth sanctify you. Exodus 31:13. And it shall come to pass, that from one new moon to another, and from one sabbath to another, shall all flesh come to worship before me, saith the LORD. Isaiah 66:23.

130 Rock Was Christ
1 Corinthians 10:1-4

131 Sacrifice and Offering
Psalm 40:5,6

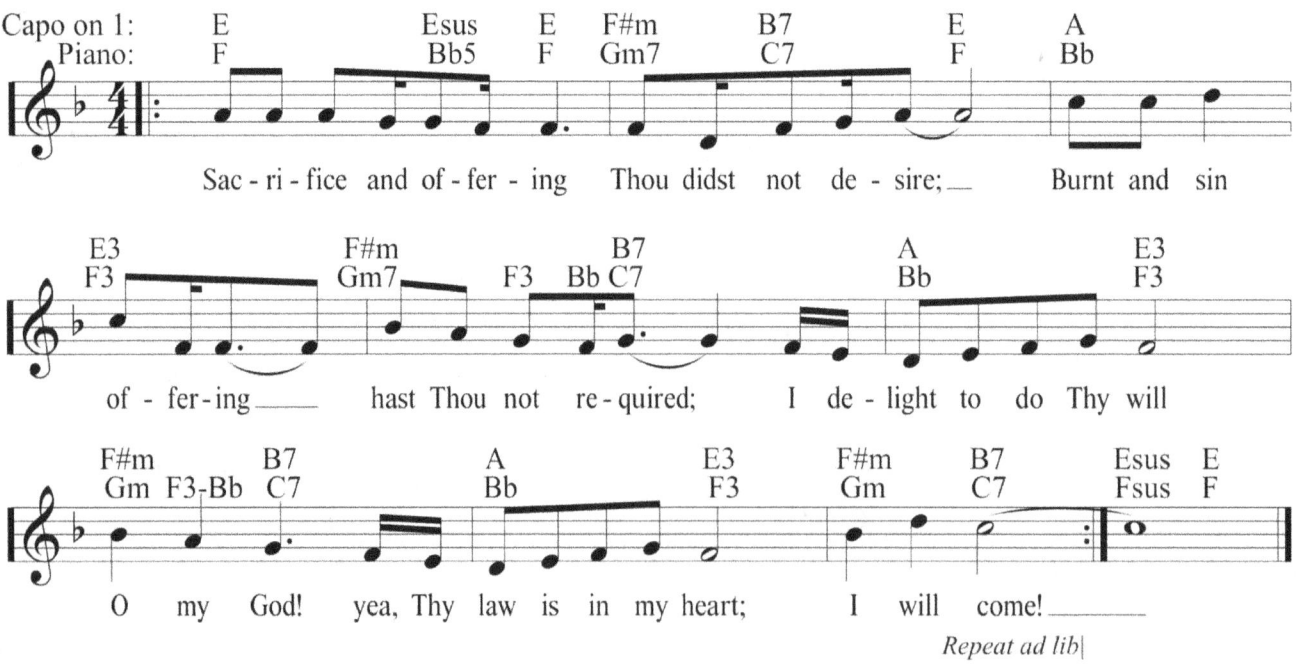

Sanctify the Lord God 132

1Peter 3:15

Saved by His Life 133

Romans 5:6-8,10

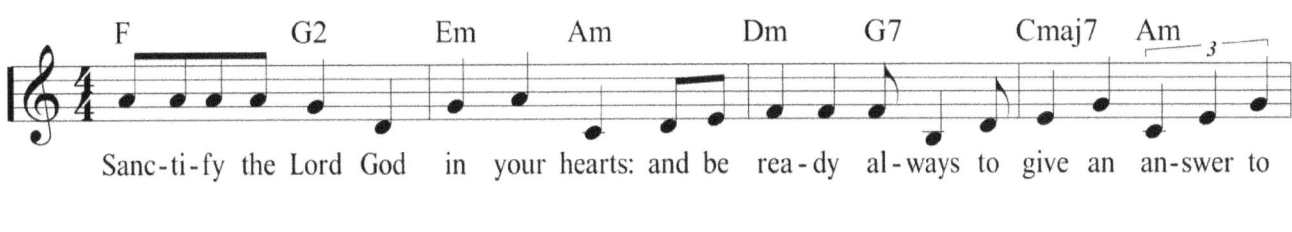

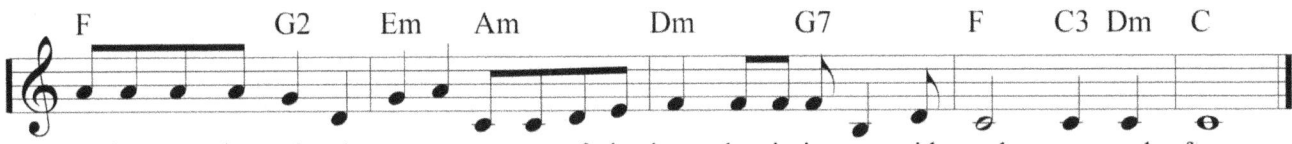

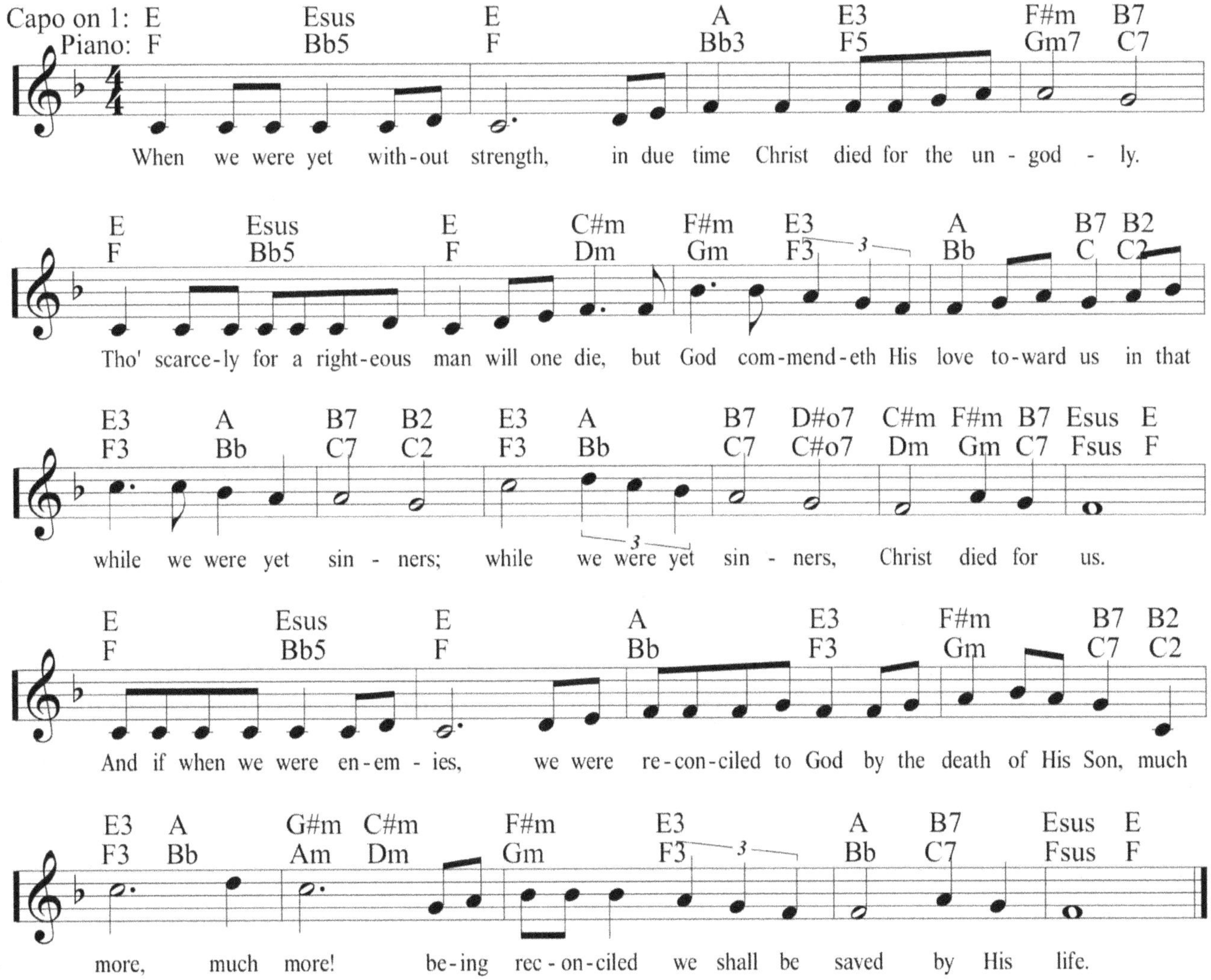

134 Search Me, O God

Psalm 139:23,24

135 Search the Scriptures

John 5:39; 2 Timothy 3:16,17

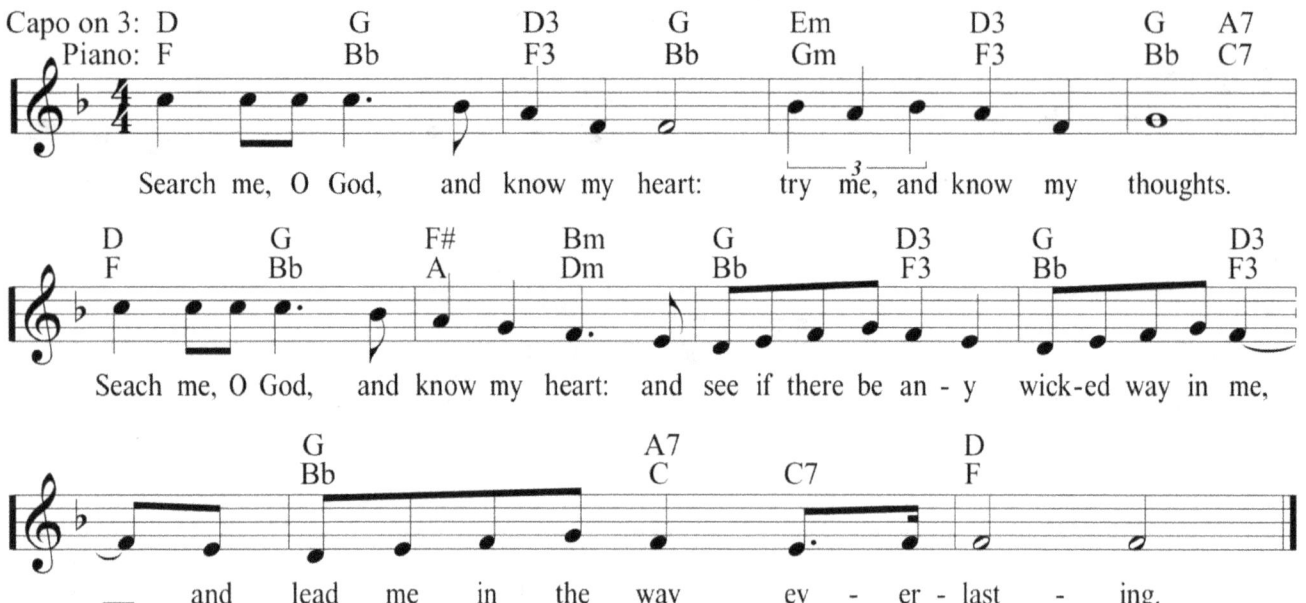

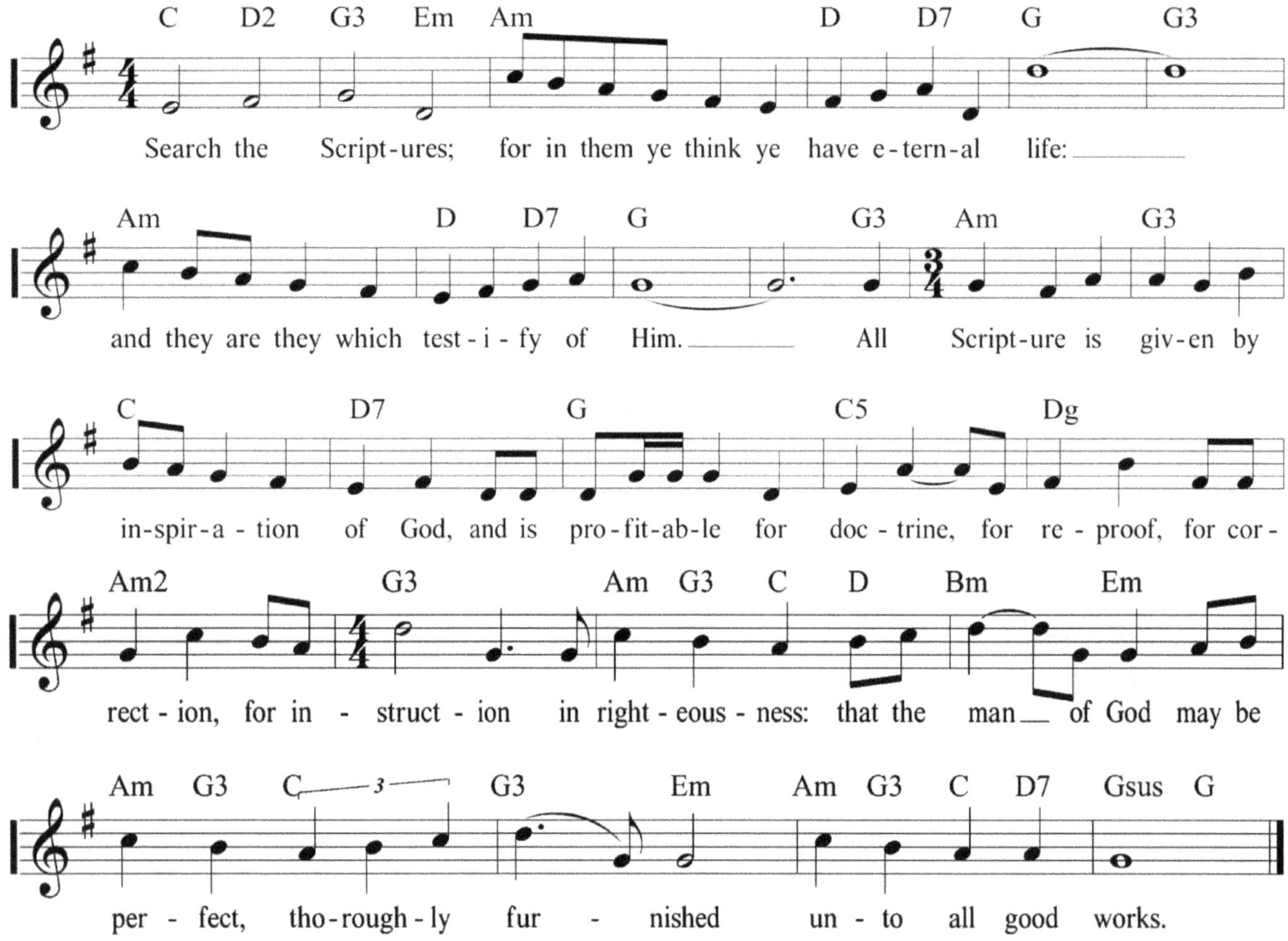

Seek Ye the Lord
Isaiah 55:6,7
136

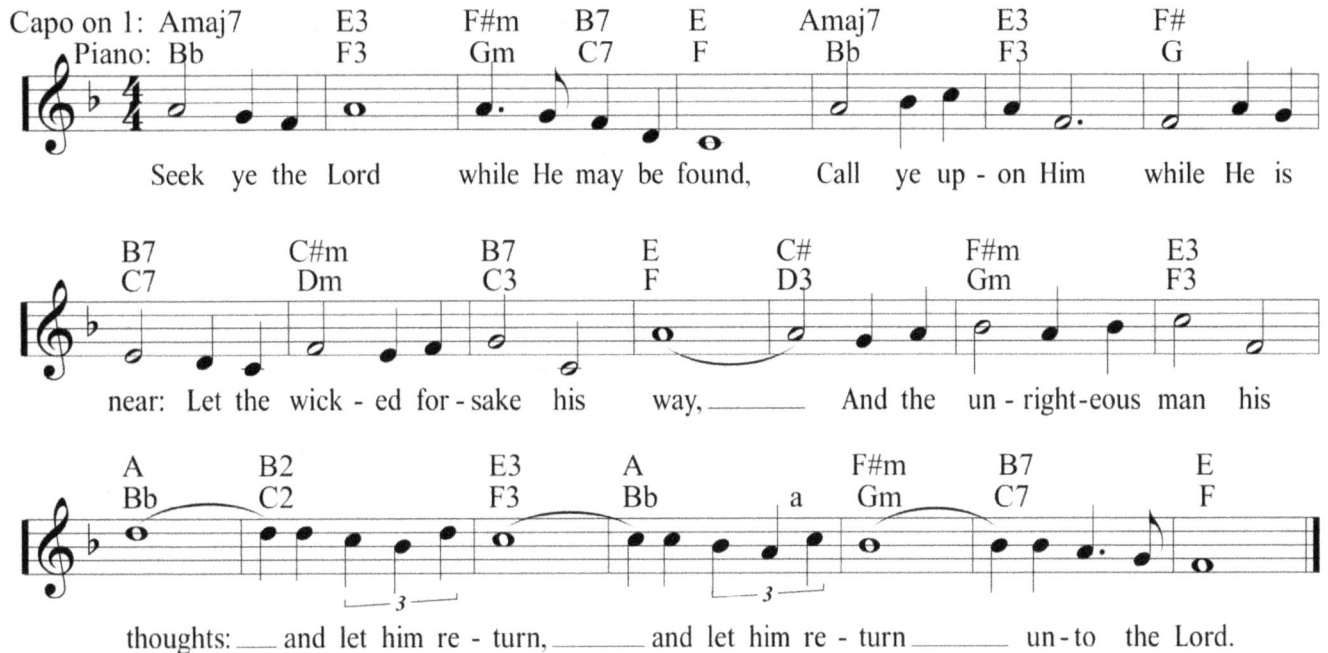

Set Me as a Seal
Song of Solomon 8:6
137

138 Stand Ye in the Ways
Jeremiah 6:16

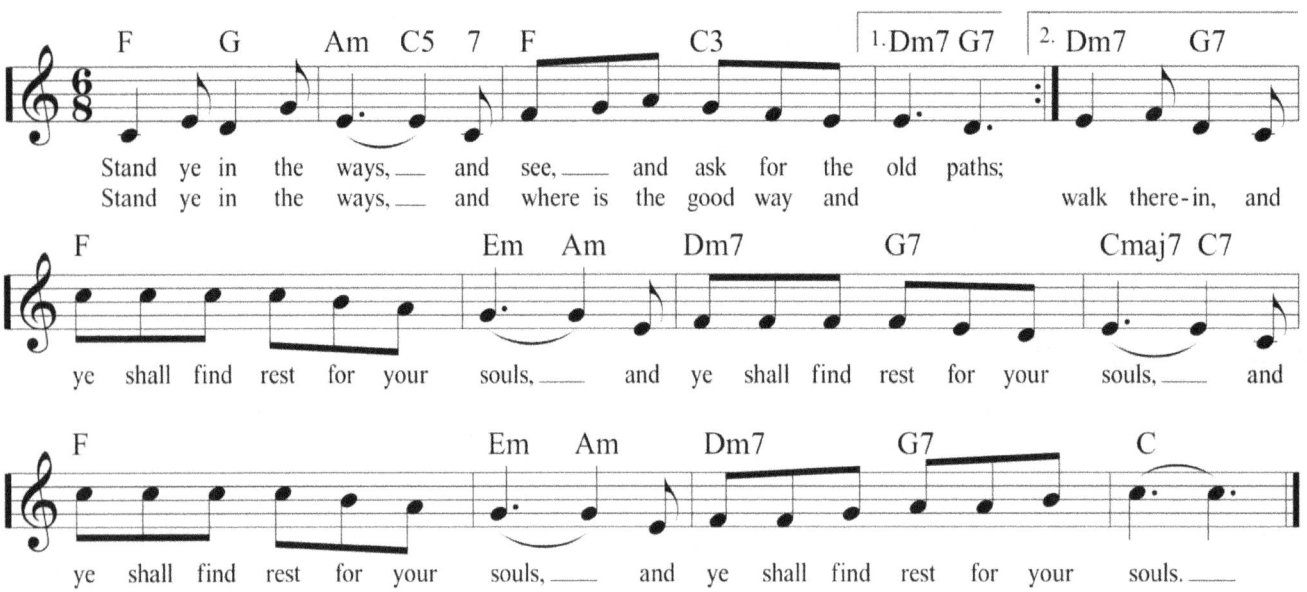

139 Submit Yourselves
James 4:7,8

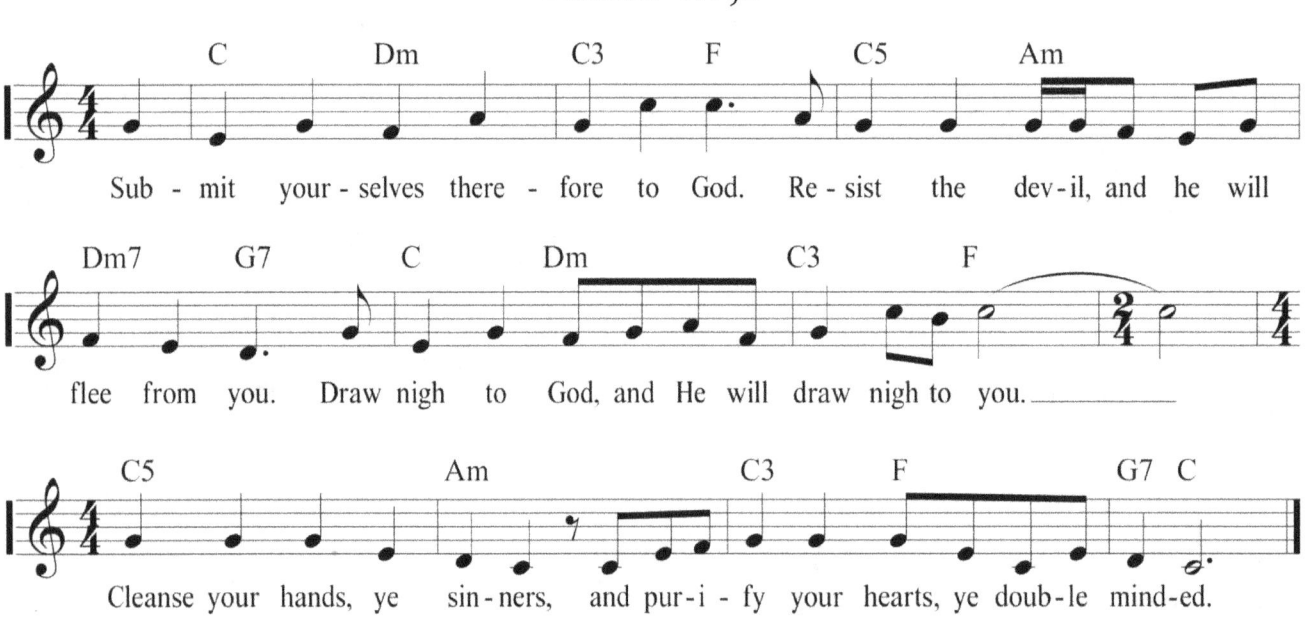

Suffer Little Children 140
Matthew 19:14

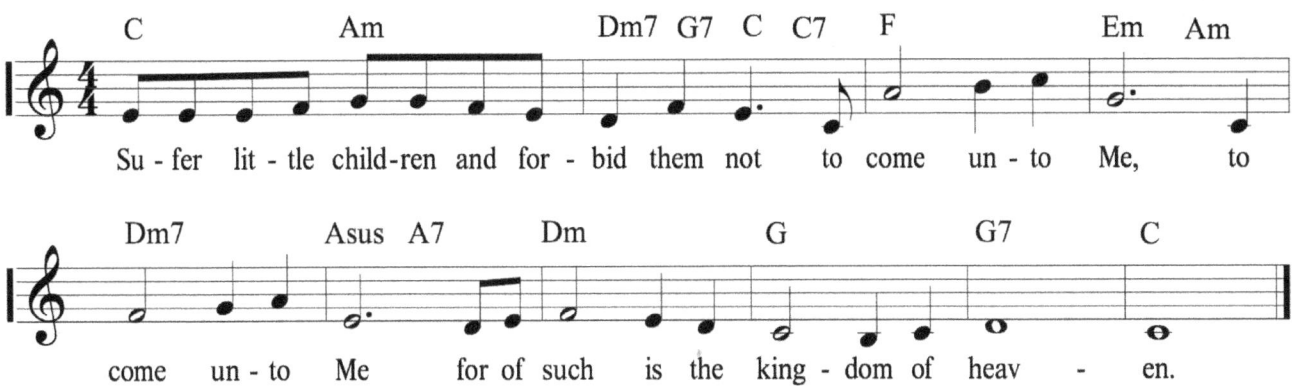

Sun Shall Be No More 141
Isaiah 60:19

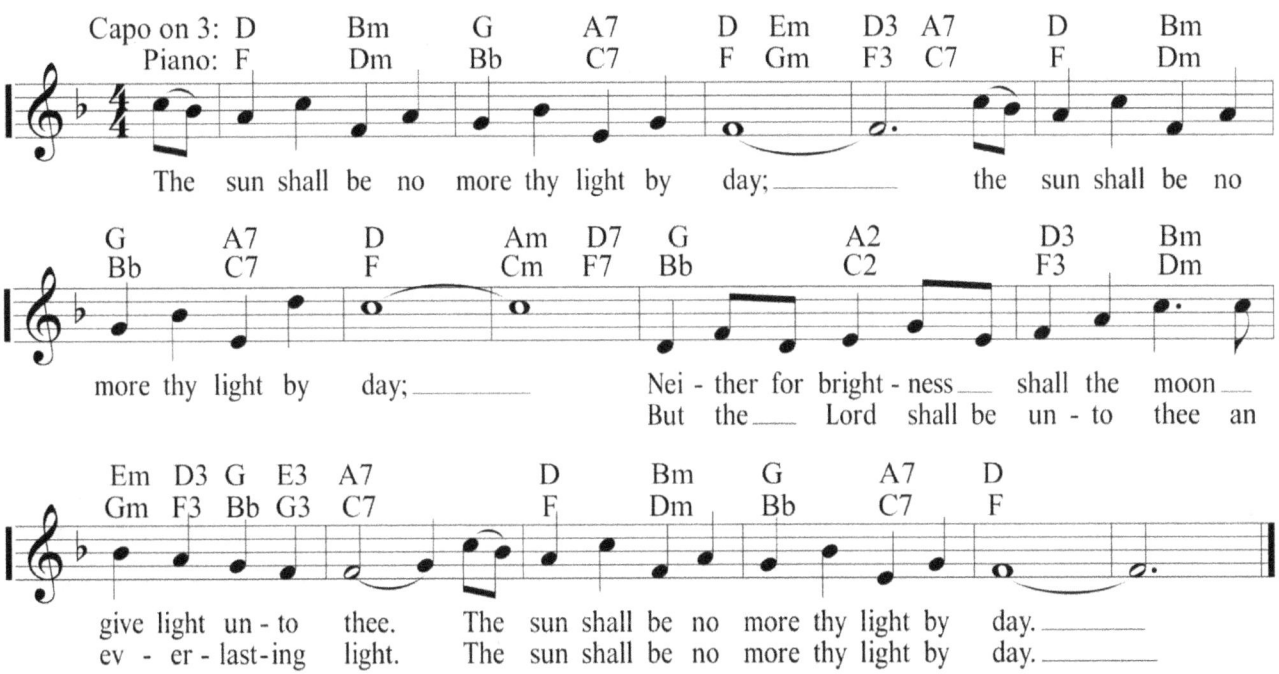

The light of the moon shall be as the light of the sun, and the light of the sun shall be sevenfold, as the light of seven days, in the day that the LORD bindeth up the breach of His people, and healeth the stroke of their wound. Isaiah 30:26. And the city had no need of the sun, neither of the moon, to shine in it: for the glory of God did lighten it, and the Lamb is the light thereof. Revelation 21:23.

142 Then Shall We Know

Hosea 6:3

143 Then They That Feared the Lord

Malachi 3:16

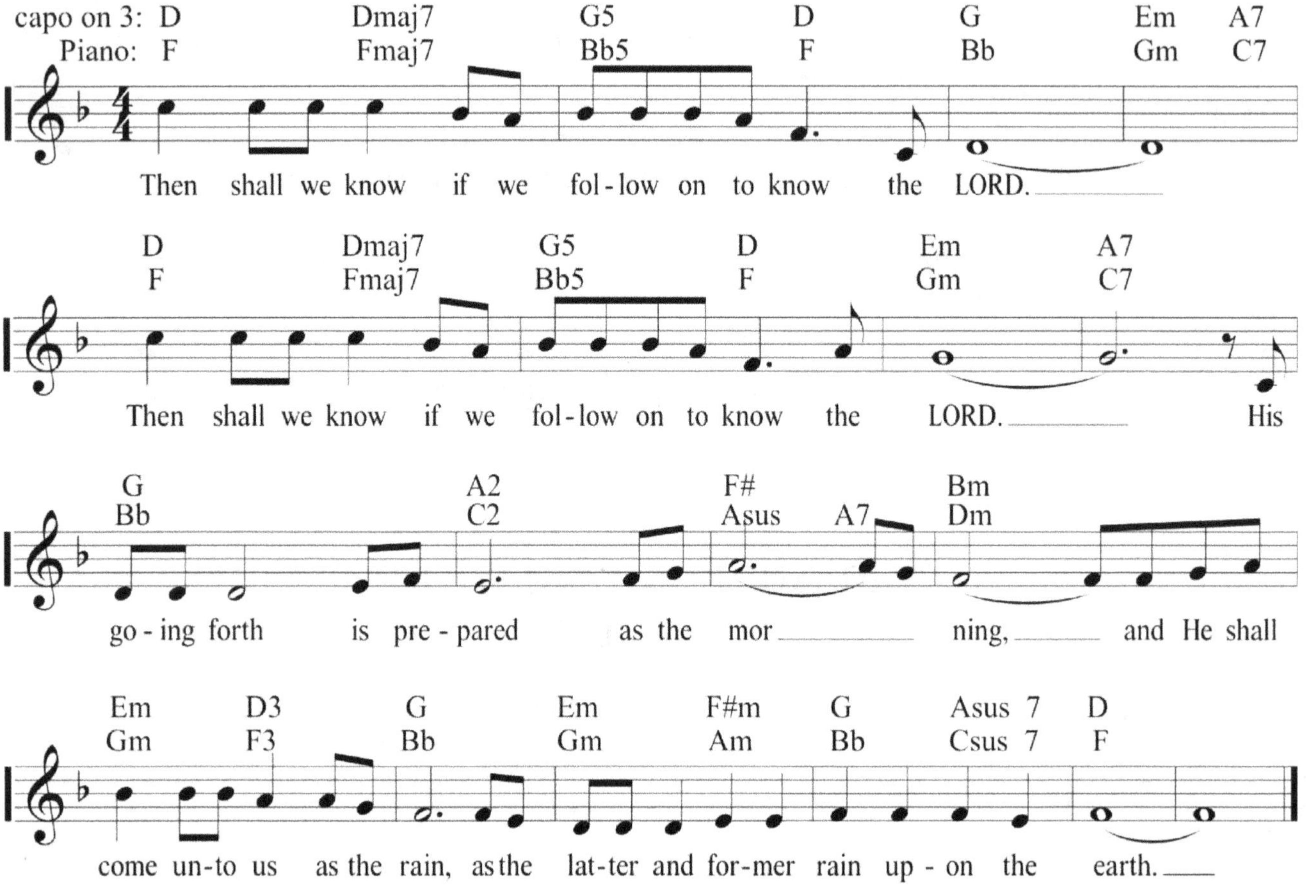

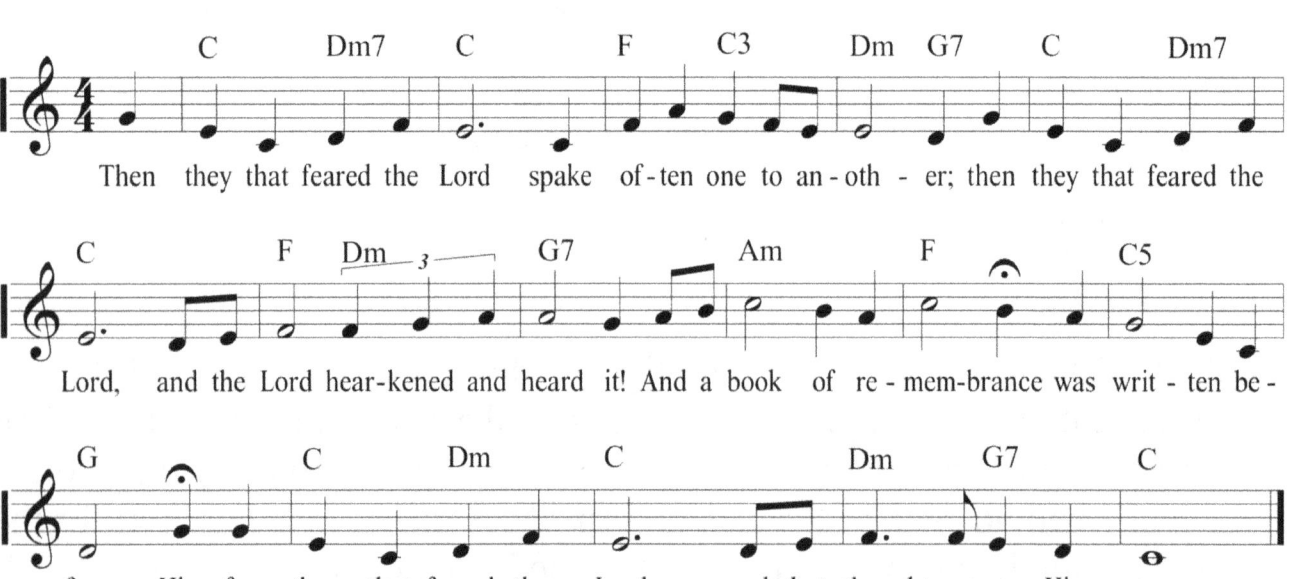

There is One God
1 Timothy 2:5
144

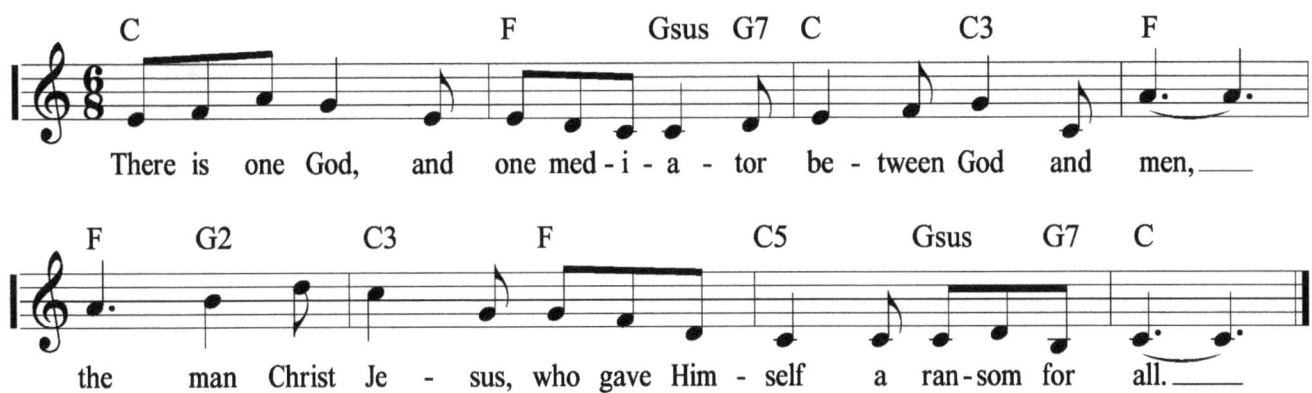

There is one God, the Father of whom are all things and we in Him; and one Lord Jesus Christ, by whom are all things and we by him. 1Corinthians 8:6. One God and Father of all, who is above all, and through all, and in you all. Ephesians 4:6. Master, Thou hast said the truth: for there is one God; and there is none other but He. Mark 12:32. Thou believest that there is one God; thou doest well: the devils also believe and tremble. James 2:19.

Think On These Things
Philippians 4:8
145

146 This I Confess unto You
Acts 24:14,15

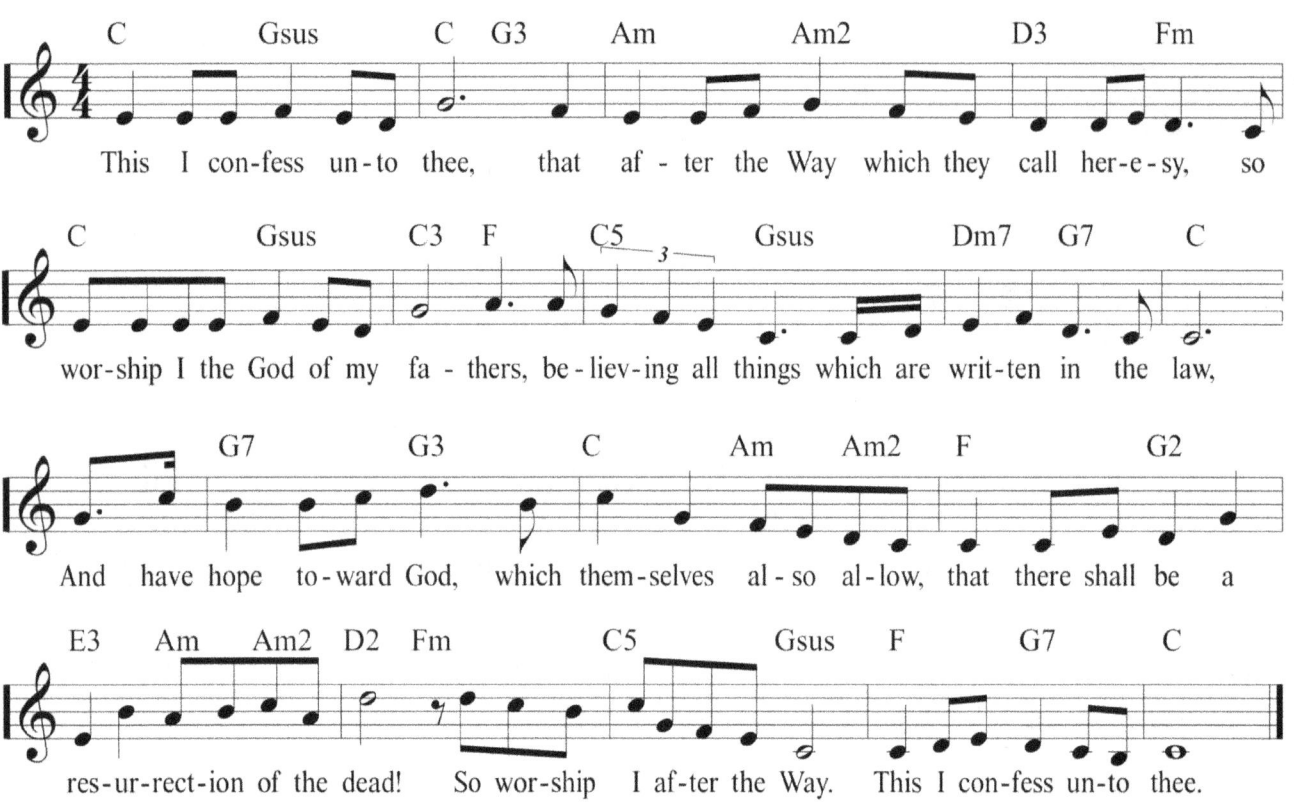

147 This is My Beloved Son
Matthew 17:5

This is the Covenant
Hebrews 8:10
148

This is the Way
Isaiah 30:21
149

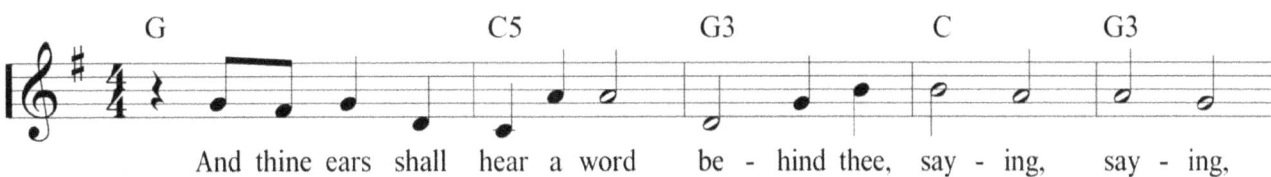

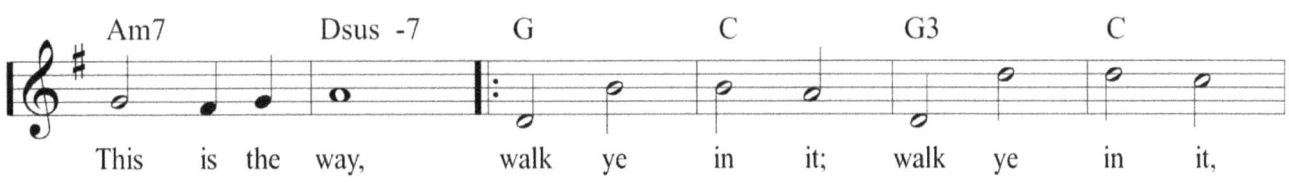

150 This One Thing I Do
Philippians 3:13,14

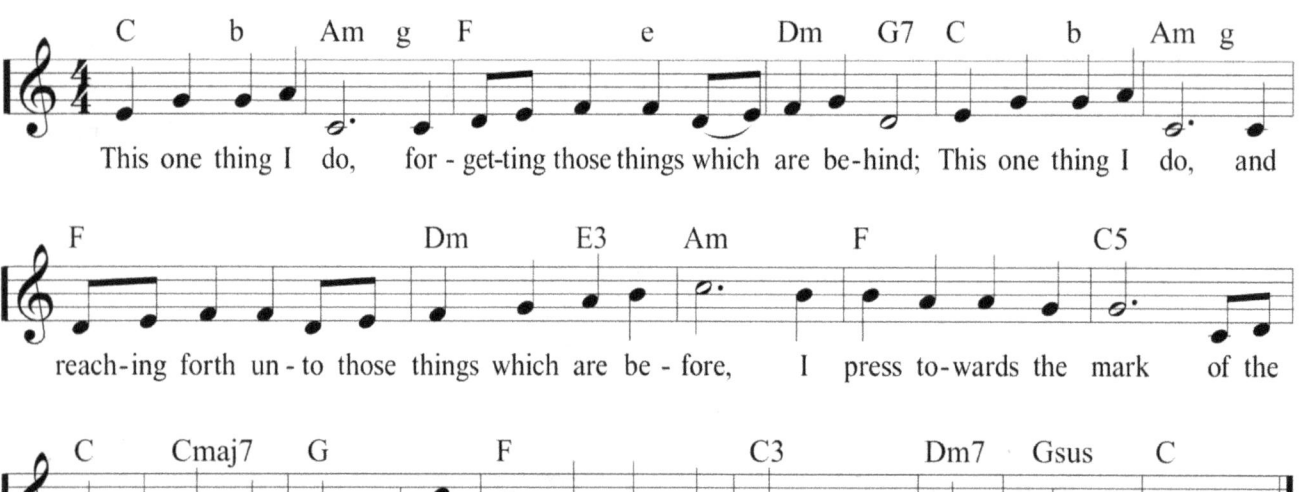

151 Thou Art My Son
Psalm 2:1,2, 6-8

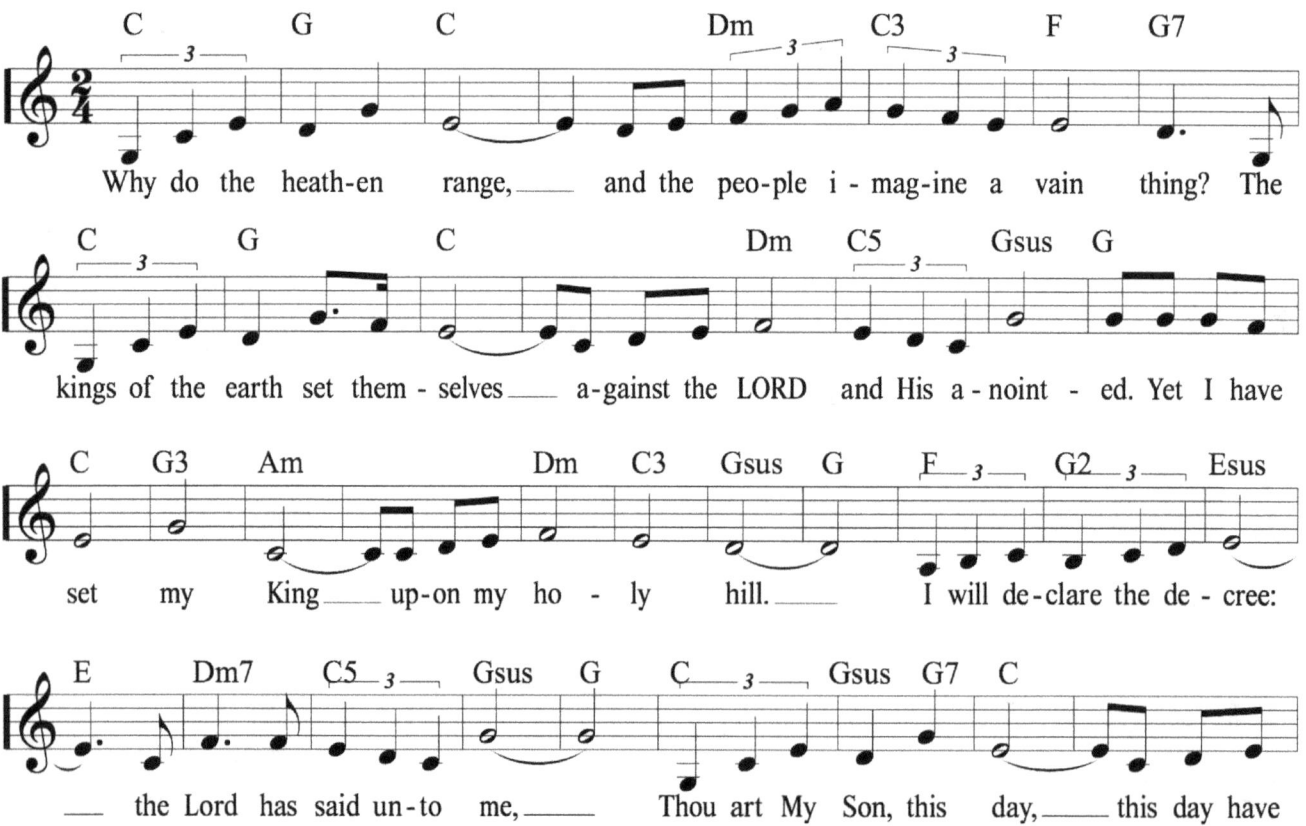

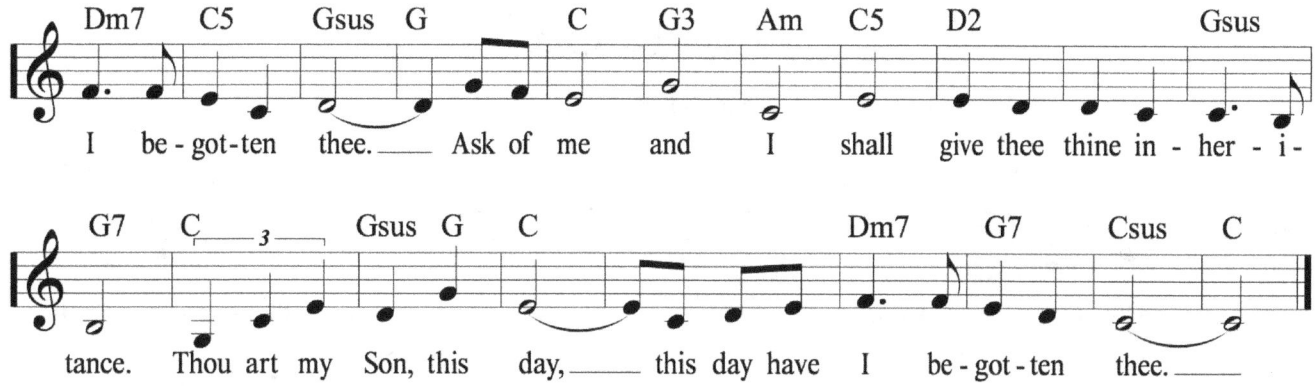

When He bringeth in the firstbegotten into the world, He said, And let all the angels of God worship him. Hebrews 1:6. God sent His only begotten Son into the world, that we might live through him. 1John 4:9. No man hath seen God at any time, the only begotten Son, which is in the bosom of the Father, he hath declared Him. John 1:18.

Thy Maker is Thine Husband 152
Isaiah 54:5

I have espoused you to one husband, that I may present you as a chaste virgin to Christ. 2Corinthians 11:2 For this cause shall a man leave his father and mother, and shall be joined unto his wife, and they two shall be one flesh. This is a great mystery: but I speak concerning Christ and the church. Ephesians 5:31,32 The marriage of the Lamb is come, and His wife hath made herself ready. Revelation 19:7

153 Thy Throne O God

Psalm 45:6,7

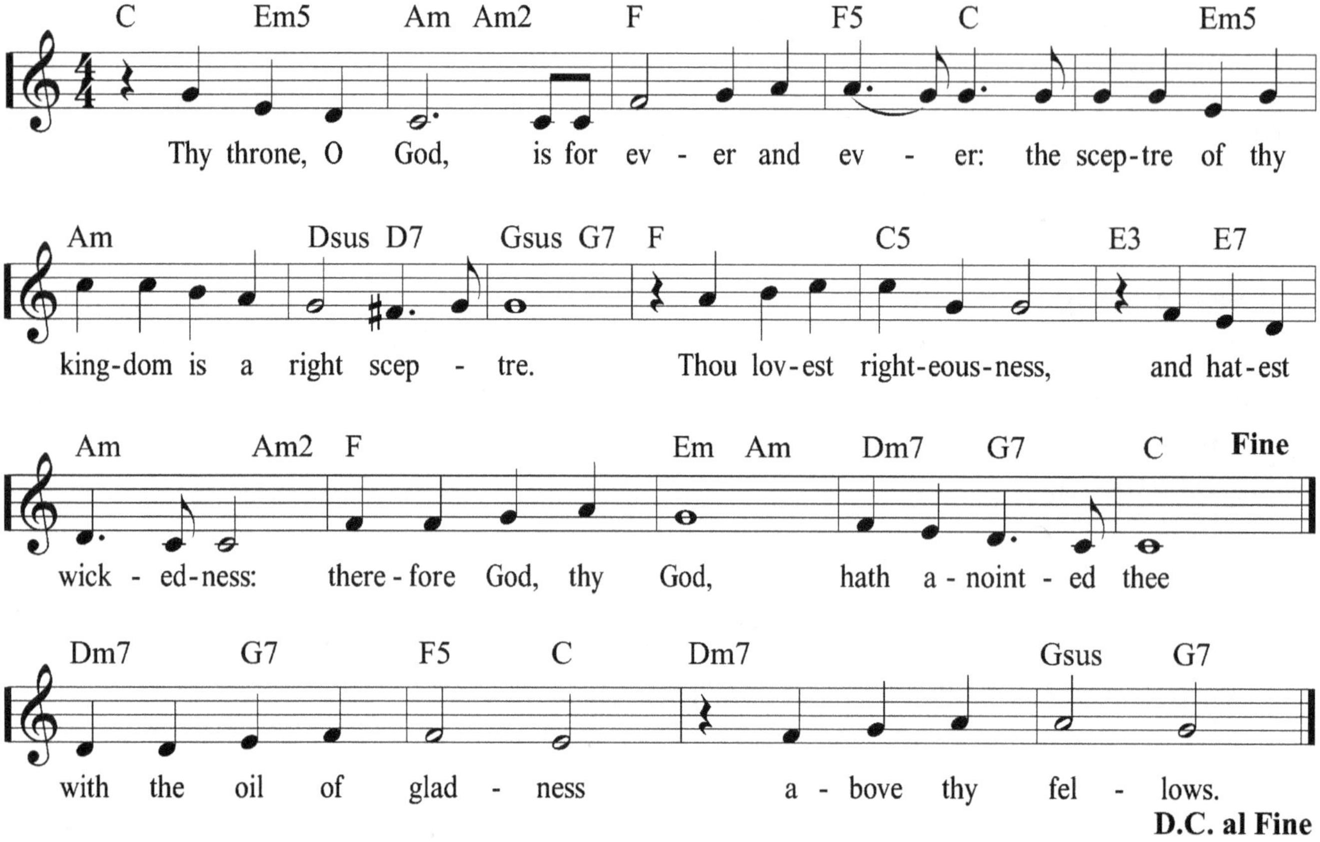

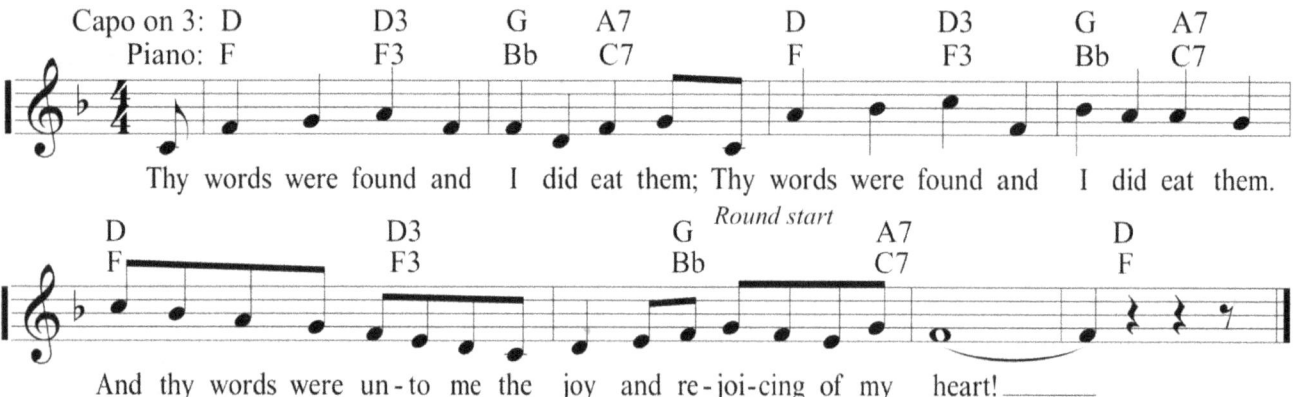

C Em5 Am Am2 F F5 C Em5
Thy throne, O God, is for ev - er and ev - er: the scep-tre of thy
Am Dsus D7 Gsus G7 F C5 E3 E7
king-dom is a right scep - tre. Thou lov-est right-eous-ness, and hat-est
Am Am2 F Em Am Dm7 G7 C
Fine
wick - ed-ness: there - fore God, thy God, hath a - noint - ed thee
Dm7 G7 F5 C Dm7 Gsus G7
with the oil of glad - ness a - bove thy fel - lows.
D.C. al Fine

154 Thy Words Were Found

Jeremiah 15:16

Capo on 3: D D3 G A7 D D3 G A7
Piano: F F3 Bb C7 F F3 Bb C7
Thy words were found and I did eat them; Thy words were found and I did eat them.
D D3 G A7 D
F F3 Bb C7 F
Round start
And thy words were un-to me the joy and re-joi-cing of my heart!

Son of man, eat that thou findest; eat this roll, and go speak unto the house of Israel. So I opened my mouth, and he caused me to eat that roll. And he said unto me, Son of man, cause thy belly to eat, and fill thy bowels with this roll that I give thee. Then did I eat it; and it was in my mouth as honey for sweetness. Ezekiel 3:1-3. And I took the little book out of the angel's hand, and ate it up; and it was in my mouth sweet as honey: and as soon as I had eaten it, my belly was bitter. Revelation 10:10.

Till We All Come In
Ephesians 4:13

155

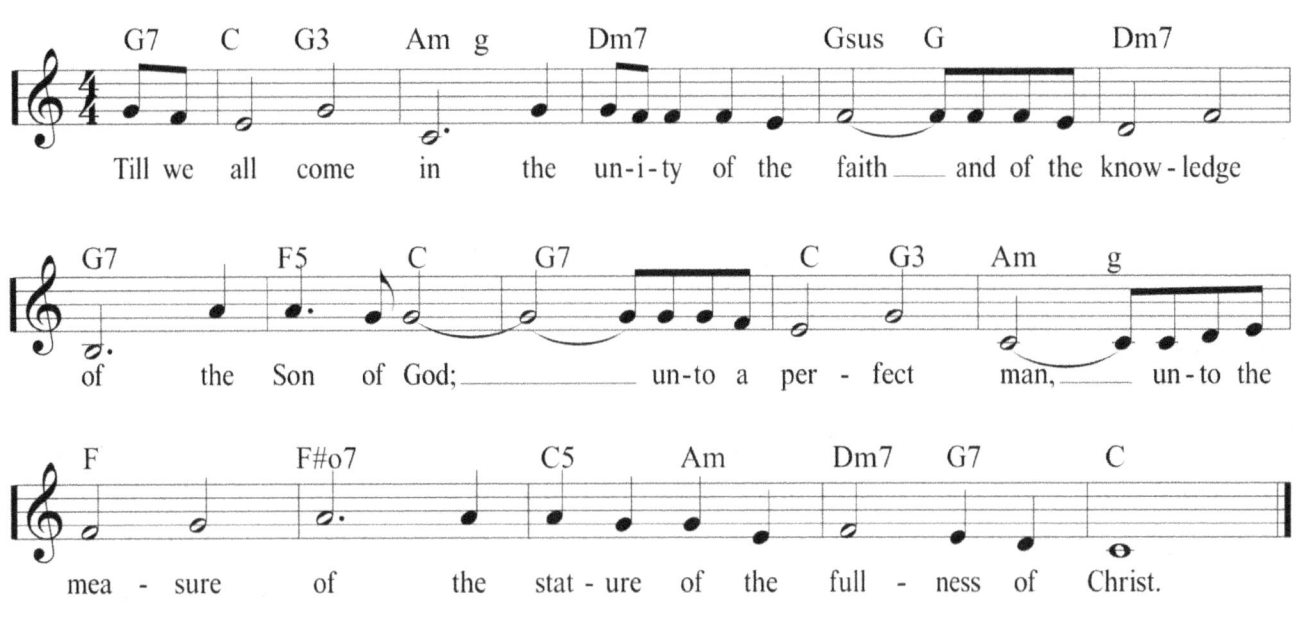

Till we all come in the un-i-ty of the faith and of the know-ledge of the Son of God; un-to a per-fect man, un-to the mea-sure of the stat-ure of the full-ness of Christ.

To Live is Christ
Philippians 1:19-21

156

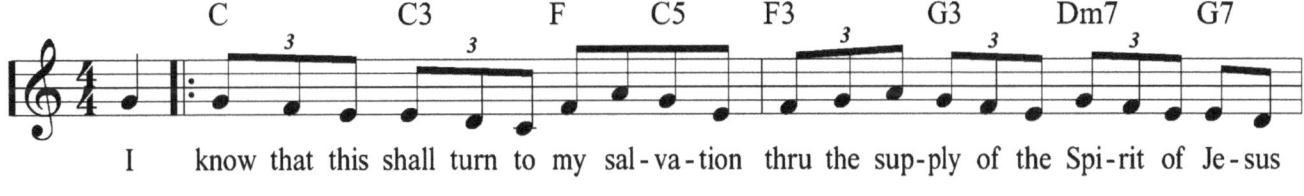

I know that this shall turn to my sal-va-tion thru the sup-ply of the Spi-rit of Je-sus

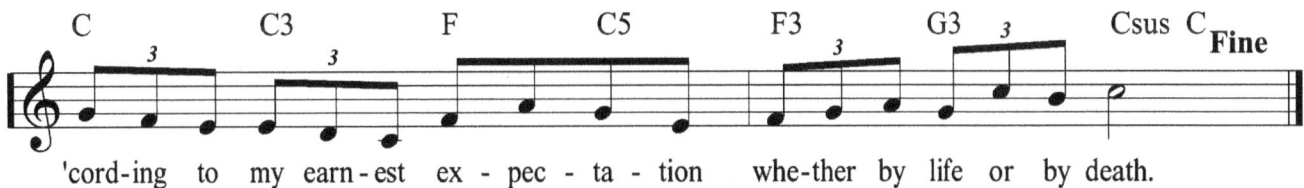

'cord-ing to my earn-est ex-pec-ta-tion whe-ther by life or by death.

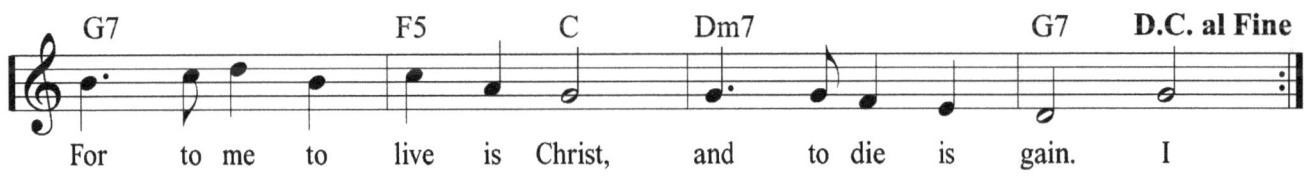

For to me to live is Christ, and to die is gain. I

The testimony of Jesus is the Spirit of prophecy. Revelation 19:10. The prophets have enquired and searched diligently…what manner of time the Spirit of Christ which was in them did signify, when it testified beforehand the sufferings of Christ. 1Peter 1:10,11.

157 Truly Our Fellowship
1 John 1:3

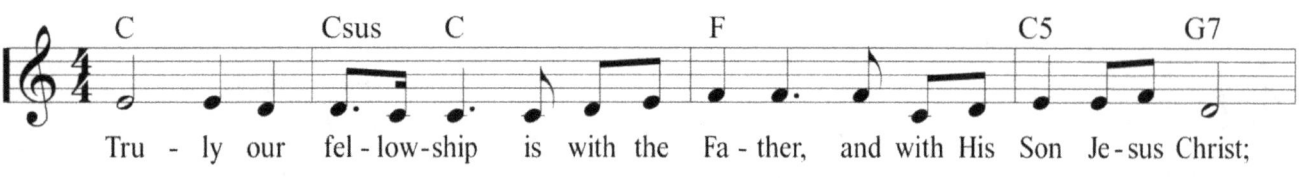

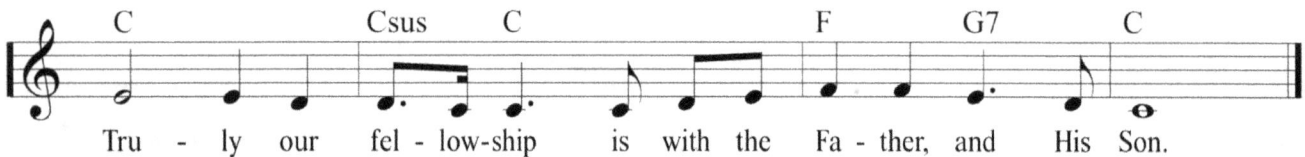

He is antichrist, that denieth the Father and the Son. Whosoever denieth the Son, the same hath not the Father: he that acknowledgeth the Son hath the Father also. Let that therefore abide in you, which ye have heard from the beginning. If that which ye have heard from the beginning shall remain in you, ye also shall continue in the Son, and in the Father. 1John 2:22-24.

158 We Have Such an High Priest
Hebrews 8:1

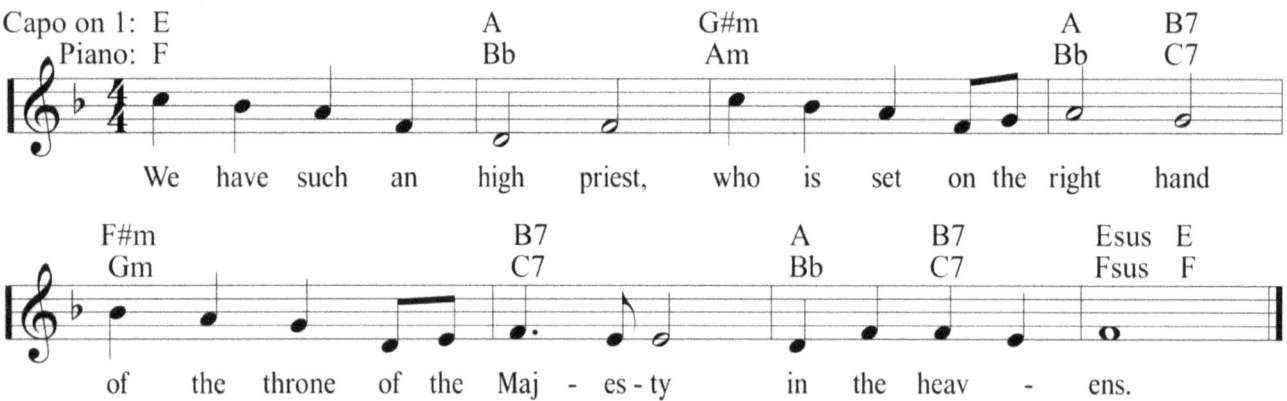

Seeing then that we have a great high priest, that is passed into the heavens, Jesus the Son of God, let us hold fast our profession. For we have not an high priest which cannot be touched with the feelings of our infirmities; but was in all points tempted like as we are, yet without sin. Hebrews 4:14,15.

What is a Man Profited?   159
Matthew 16:26

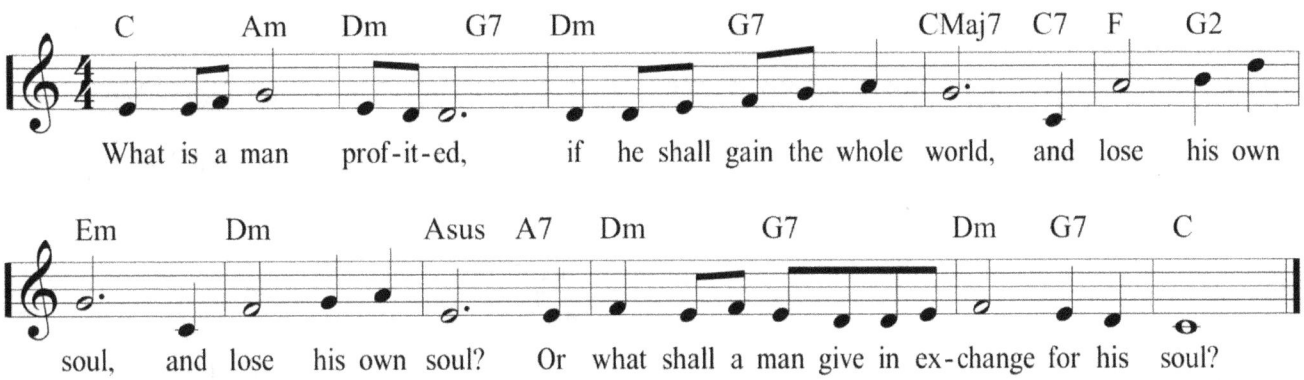

What is His Name?   160
Proverbs 30:4

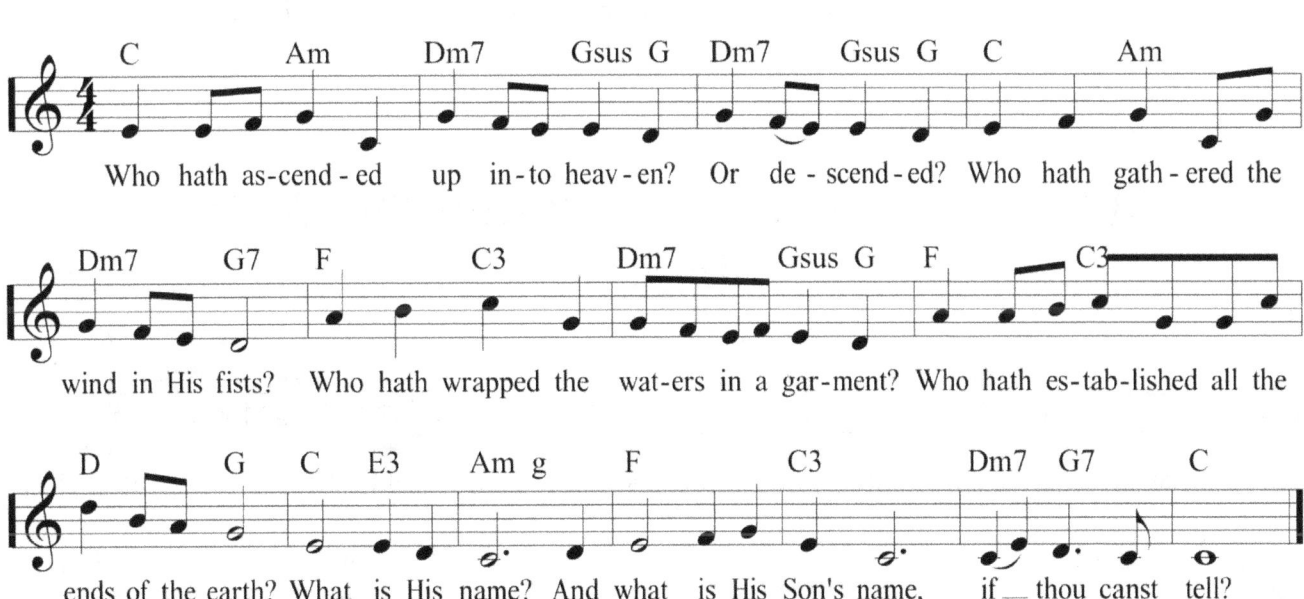

Jesus answered them, My Father worketh hitherto, and I work. Therefore the Jews sought the more to kill him, because he not only had broken the sabbath, but said also that God was his Father, making himself equal with God. John 5:17,18. I am come in my Father's name. John 5:43.

161 When Christ Who is Our Life
Colossians 3:4; 1 John 3:2

162 When Thou Passest Through the Waters
Isaiah 43:2,3

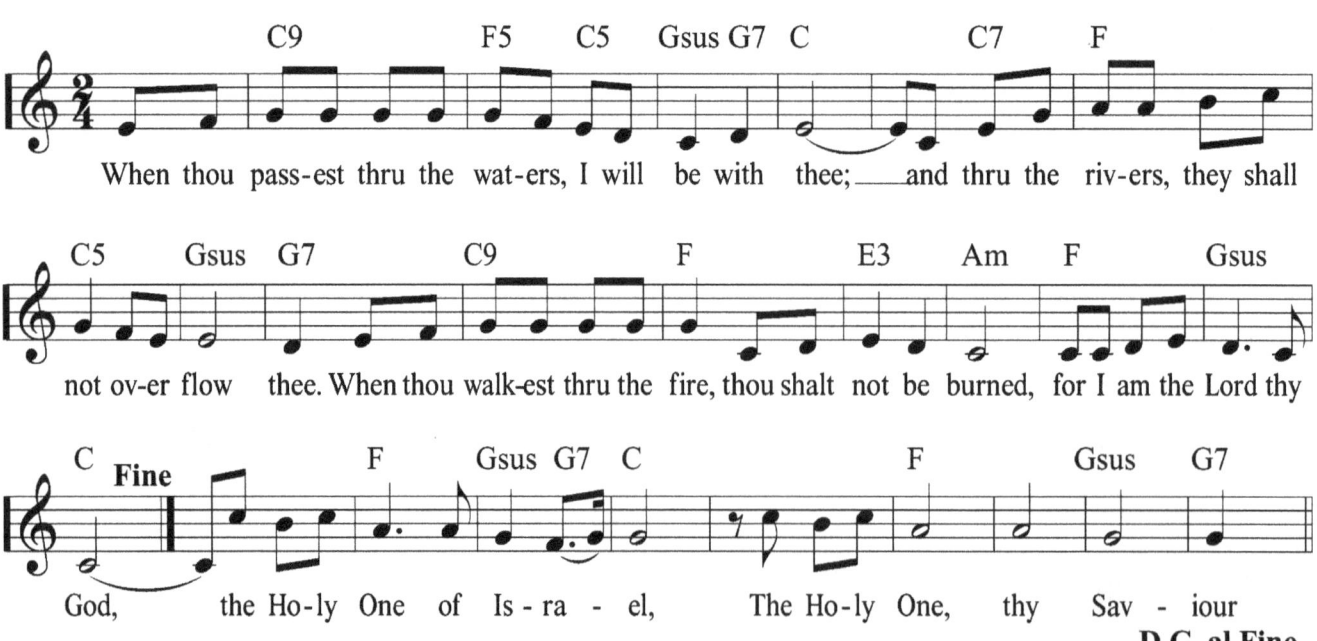

D.C. al Fine

Whither Shall I Go? 163
Psalm 139:7-10

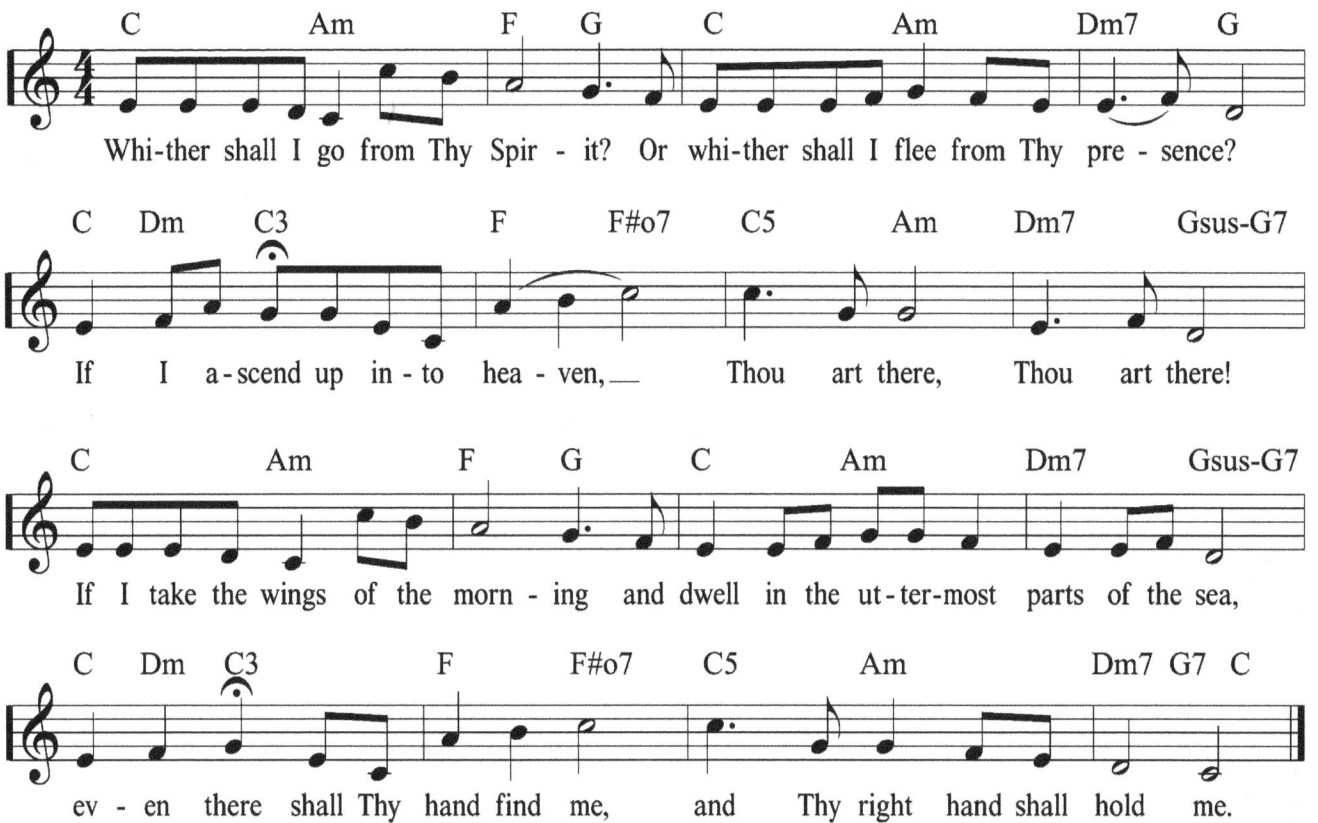

My presence shall go with thee, and I will give you rest. Exodus 33:14. In thy presence is fulness of joy; at thy right hand there are pleasures for evermore. Psalm 16:11. The upright shall dwell in thy presence. Psalm 140:13.

With My Whole Heart 164
Psalm 119:10,11

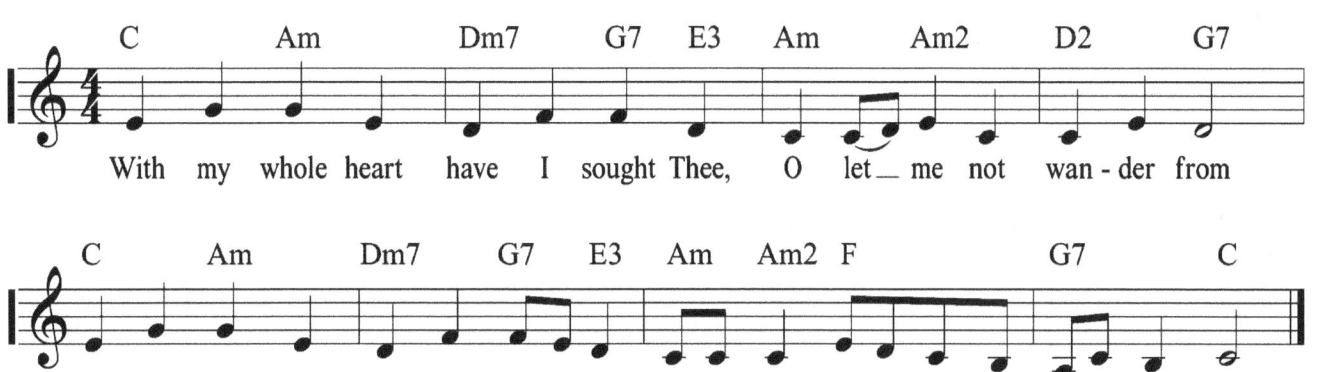

165 The Word Was Made Flesh

John 1:14; 2 Corinthians 4:11

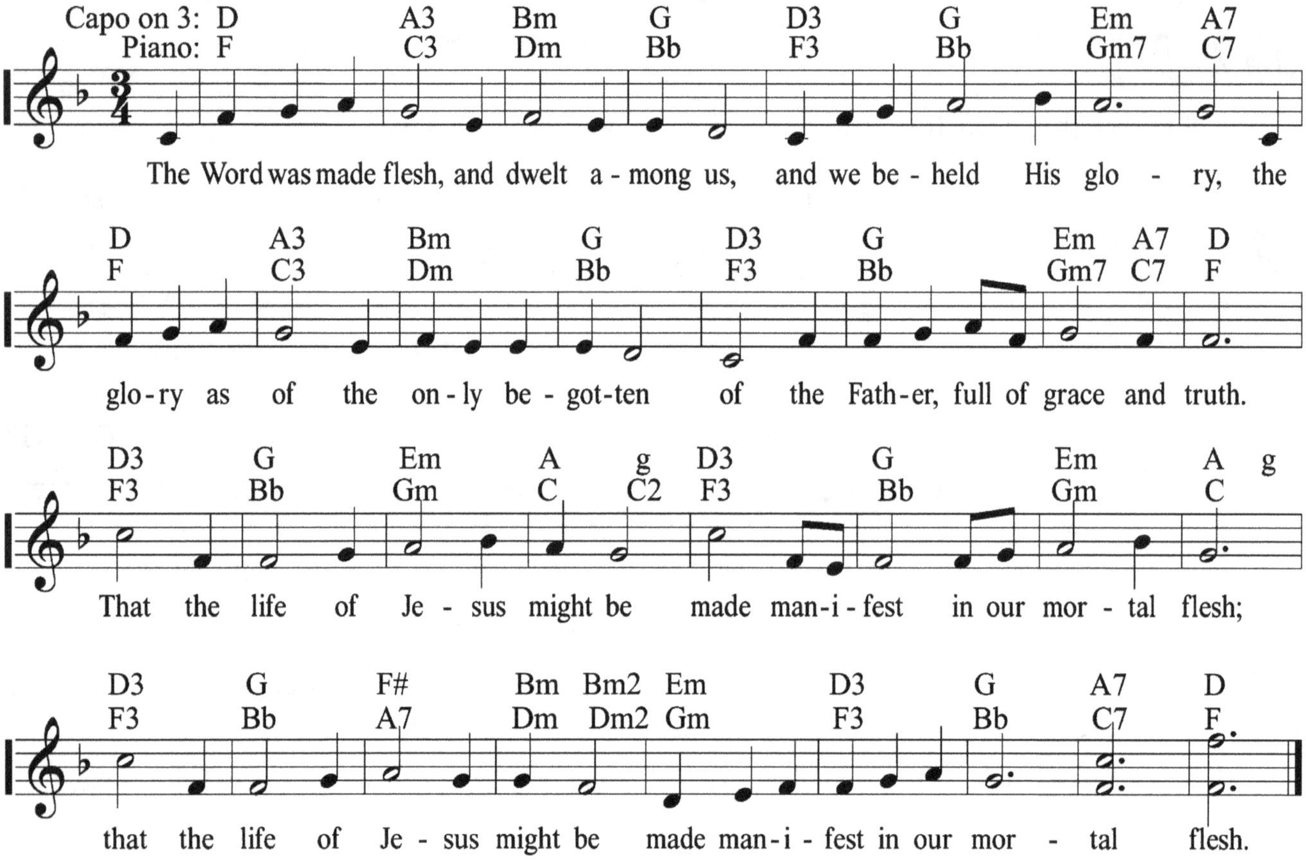
Capo on 3: D A3 Bm G D3 G Em A7
Piano: F C3 Dm Bb F3 Bb Gm7 C7
The Word was made flesh, and dwelt a - mong us, and we be - held His glo - ry, the
D A3 Bm G D3 G Em A7 D
F C3 Dm Bb F3 Bb Gm7 C7 F
glo - ry as of the on - ly be - got-ten of the Fath-er, full of grace and truth.
D3 G Em A g D3 G Em A g
F3 Bb Gm C C2 F3 Bb Gm C
That the life of Je - sus might be made man-i - fest in our mor - tal flesh;
D3 G F# Bm Bm2 Em D3 G A7 D
F3 Bb A7 Dm Dm2 Gm F3 Bb C7 F
that the life of Je - sus might be made man-i - fest in our mor - tal flesh.

166 Work Out Your Own Salvation

Philippians 2:12,13

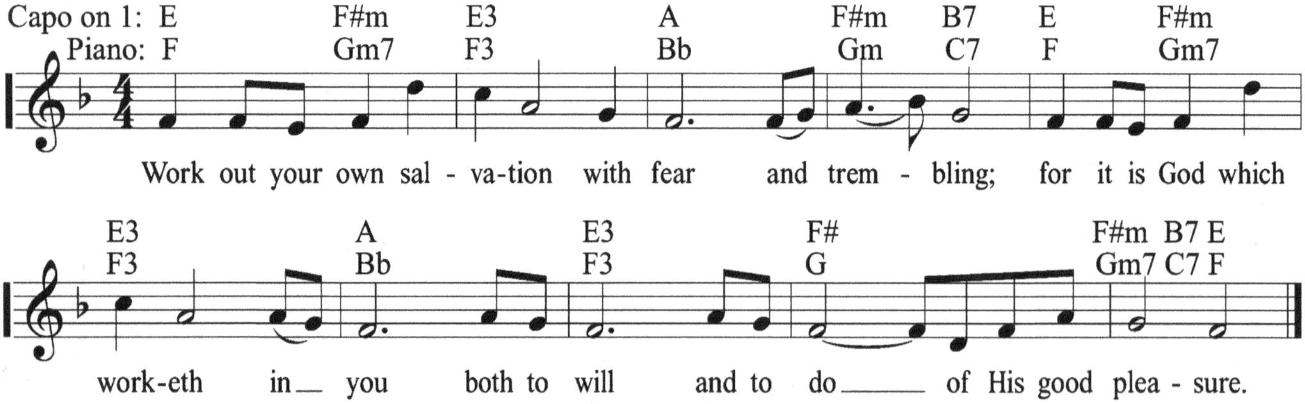
Capo on 1: E F#m E3 A F#m B7 E F#m
Piano: F Gm7 F3 Bb Gm C7 F Gm7
Work out your own sal - va-tion with fear and trem - bling; for it is God which
E3 A E3 F# F#m B7 E
F3 Bb F3 G Gm7 C7 F
work-eth in you both to will and to do of His good plea - sure.

Ye Men of Galilee 167
Acts 1:11

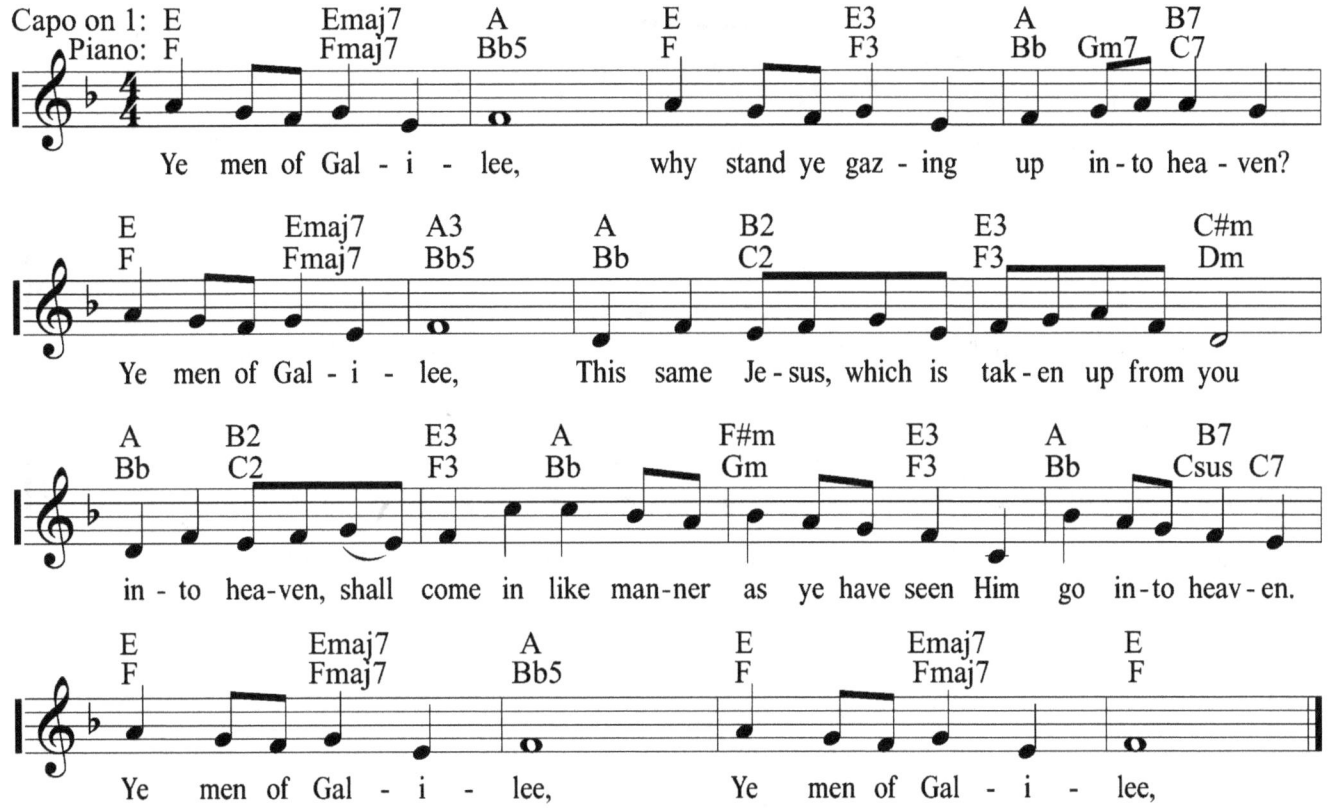

Ye Shall Be Clean 168
Ezekiel 36:25,26

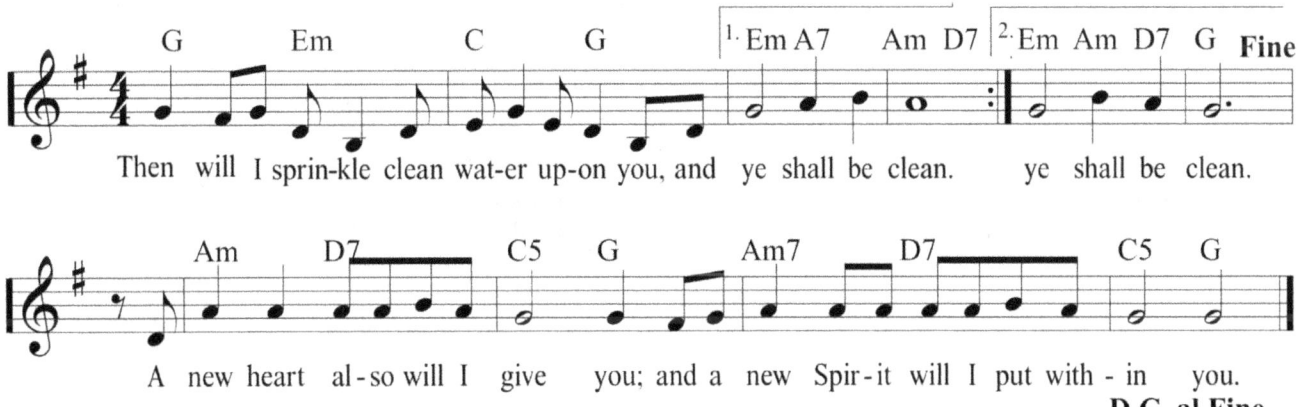

And I will take away the stony heart out of your flesh, and I will give you an heart of flesh. And I will put my spirit within you, and cause you to walk in my statutes, and ye shall keep my judgments, and do them. Ezekiel 36:26,27.

169 Ye Shall Seek Me and Find Me
Jeremiah 29:13,14,11

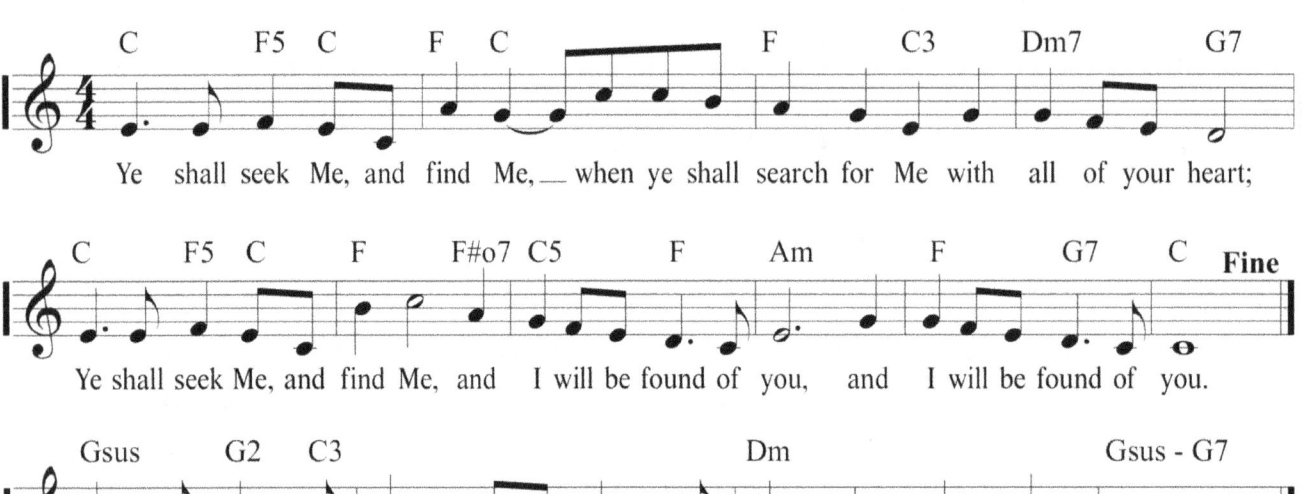

170
Jeremiah 29:13

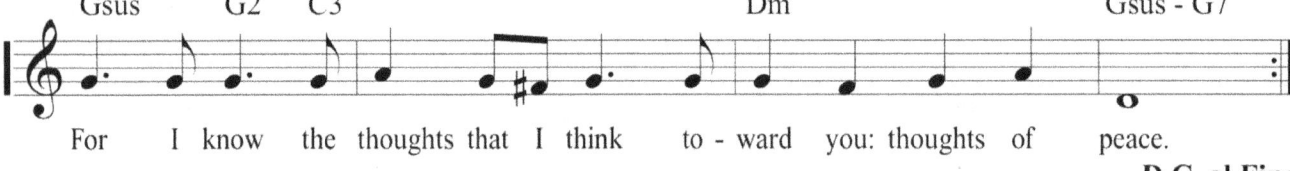

Music by Alexandra Hullquist

Then shall ye call upon Me,
and ye shall go and pray unto me,
and I will hearken unto you.
                        Jeremiah 29:12.

Praise ye the LORD.
Praise God in his sanctuary:
Praise him in the firmament of his power.
Praise him for his mighty acts:
Praise him according to his excellent greatness.
Praise him with the sound of the trumpet:
Praise him with the psaltery and harp.
Praise him with the timbrel and dance:
Praise him with stringed instruments and organs.
Praise him upon the loud cymbals:
Praise him upon the high sounding cymbals.
Let everything that hath breath praise the LORD.
Praise ye the LORD.

Psalm 150

Directions For Singing

(From John Wesley's *Select Hymns*, 1761)

1. Learn these tunes before you learn any others; afterwards learn as many as you please.
2. Sing them exactly as they are printed here, without altering or mending them at all; and if you have learned to sing them otherwise, unlearn it as soon as you can.
3. Sing all. See that you join with the congregation as frequently as you can. Let not a slight degree of weakness or weariness hinder you If it is a cross to you, take it up, and you will find it a blessing.
4. Sing lustily and with good courage. Beware of singing as if you were half dead, or half asleep; but lift up your voice with strength. Be no more afraid of your voice now, nor more ashamed of its being heard, than when you sung the songs of Satan.
5. Sing modestly. Do not bawl, so as to be heard above or distinct from the rest of the congregation, that you may not destroy the harmony; but strive to unite your voices together, so as to make one clear melodious sound.
6. Sing in time. Whatever time is sung be sure to keep with it. Do not run before nor stray behind it; but attend close to the leading voices, and move therewith as exactly as you can: and take care not to sing too slow. This drawling way naturally steals on all who are lazy; and it is high time to drive it out from us, and sing all our tunes just as quick as we did at first.
7. Above all sing spiritually. Have an eye to God in every word you sing. Aim at pleasing him more than yourself, or any other creature. In order to do this attend strictly to the sense of what you sing, and see that your heart is not carried away with the sound, but offered to God continually: so shall your singing be such as the Lord will approve here, and reward you when he cometh in the clouds of heaven.

Piano Keyboard Chord Chart

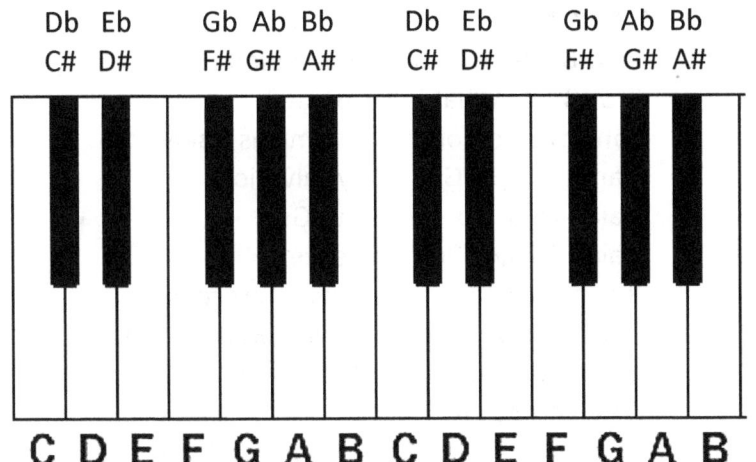

Chords listed in this book consist of the notes listed to the right of each chord. Occasionally an additional note is added to the chord abbreviation. For example Dmc# is the Dm chord (DFA) with the added c# note.

b, g, e, etc. Bass Notes

Guitar Chords

Thumb plucks strings 1-3; index finger on string 4; middle finger on string 5; ring finger string 6

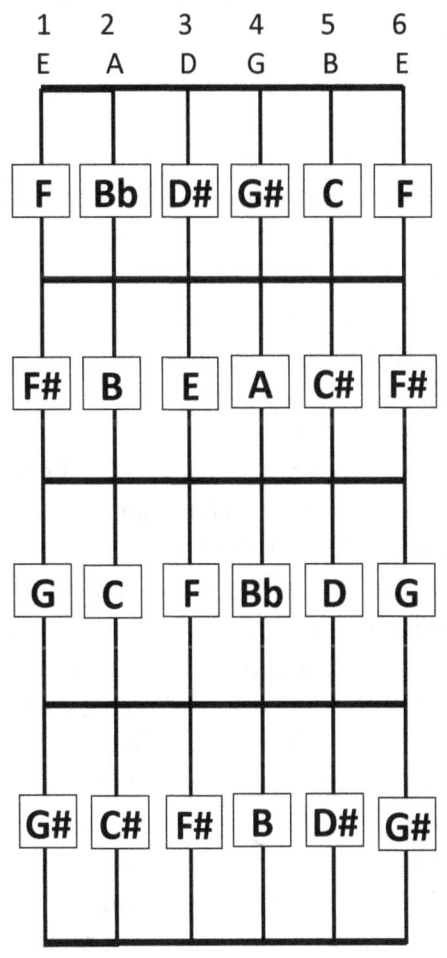

C	CEG	G	GBD	C#o7	C#EGBb	
C2	BbCEG	G2	FGBD	F#o7	F#ACD#	
C3	EGC	G3	BDG	Bo7	BDFG#	
C5	GCE	G5	DGB	Co7	CD#F#A	
C7	CEGBb	G7	GBDF	A#o7	BbEGC#	
Cmaj7	CEGB	Gm	GBbD			
C9	CDEG	Gm7	GBbDF	C75	GBbCE	
Cm	CEbG	Gsus	GACD			
Csus	CFG	G7sus	GFACD			
D	DF#A	A	AC#E	Am2	GACE	
D2	CDF#A	A2	GAC#E	Dm2	CDFA	
D3	F#AD	A3	C#EA			
D5	ADF#	A5	EAC#			
D7	DF#AC	A7	AC#EG			
Dm	DFA	Am	ACE	Dg	GDF#A	
Dm7	DFAC	Am7	ACEG	Dmc#	DFAC#	
Dsus	DGA	Asus	ADE			
E	EG#B	B	BD#F#			
E3	G#BE	B3	D#FEB			
E5	BEG#	B5	F#BD#			
E7	EG#BD	B7	BD#F#A	E37	G#BDE	
Em	EGB	Bm	BDF#	Emaj7	ED#G#B	
Esus	EAB	Bsus	BDF#			
F	FAC	Bb	BbDF	Eb	EbGBb	
F2	EbFAC	Bb3	DFBb			
F3	ACF	Bb5	FBbD			
F5	CFA	Bb7	BbDFAb			
F7	FACEb	Bbmaj7	BbDFA			
Fmaj7	FACE	Bbm	BbDbF	Fmaj79	FACEG	
Fm	FAbC					
Fsus	FGA					

97

Scripture Index

Exo 15:26   If thou wilt diligently hearken
Exo 20:8-11   Remember the Sabbath day
Exo 23:20,21   I send an Angel before thee
Exo 34:6,7   Lord, the Lord God merciful
Num 6:24-26   Lord bless thee and keep thee
Deut 31:6   Be strong and of good courage
Deut 32:1-4   Give ear O ye heavens
Joshua 24:15   Call upon the name of the Lord
Joshua 24:15   Choose you this day
1Kings 18:21   How long halt ye?
1Kings 18:24   Call upon the name of the Lord
1Kings 19:11,12   Behold the Lord passed by
2Chron 20:20   Believe in the Lord your God
Psalm 1:1-3   Blessed is the Man
Psalm 2:1,2,6-8   Thou art my Son
Psalm 13:2,1   Call upon the name of the Lord
Psalm 20:7,9,5   Call upon the name of the Lord
Psalm 24:7-10   Lift up your heads O ye gates
Psalm 33:6,9   By the Word of the Lord
Psalm 33:22   Let Thy mercy, O Lord, be
Psalm 34:7,8   Angel of the Lord
Psalm 37:5,6   Commit thy way unto the Lord
Psalm 40:6,8,7   Sacrifice and Offering
Psalm 45:6,7   Thy throne, O God, is forever
Psalm 46:1-3   God is our refuge and strength
Psalm 50:1-5   Mighty God, the Lord hath spoken
Psalm 51:7,9-11   Purge me with hyssop
Psalm 55:16,17   I will call upon God
Psalm 61:1-4   Lead me to the Rock
Psalm 68:4   Hallelu Jah
Psalm 86:12   I will praise Thee, O Lord my God
Psalm 90:1,2   Lord, Thou hast been
Psalm 91:1,2   He that dwelleth in the secret
Psalm 102:21,27   Call upon the name of the Lord
Psalm 107:1,2,8   O give thanks unto the Lord
Psalm 113:2,1   Call upon the name of the Lord
Psalm 116:13,17   Call upon the name of the Lord
Psalm 119:10,11   With my whole heart
Psalm 119:133,134   Order my steps in Thy word
Psalm 121:1,2   I will life up mine eyes
Psalm 121:7,8   Lord shall preserve thee
Psalm 122:1,2   Our feet shall stand
Psalm 125:2   As the mountains are round about
Psalm 128   Blessed is everyone
Psalm 133   How pleasant it is for brethren
Psalm 139:7-10   Whither shall I go?
Psalm 139:23,24   Search me, O God
Prov 8:22-24,30   Lord possessed Him
Prov 30:4   What is His name?
Song of Solomon 8:6   Set me as a seal
Isaiah 12:2,3   God is my salvation
Isaiah 25:9   Lo, this is our God
Isaiah 26:3,4   Perfect peace
Isaiah 28:9-11   Precept upon precept
Isaiah 30:21   This is the way, walk ye in it
Isaiah 40:9   Call upon the name of the Lord
Isaiah 40:31   As Eagles
Isaiah 40:26   Lift up your eyes on high
Isaiah 41:10   Fear thou not for He is with thee
Isaiah 42:16   I will bring the blind by a way
Isaiah 43:2,3   When thou passest through
Isaiah 44:3,4   I will pour water
Isaiah 44:22   He has blotted out as a thick cloud
Isaiah 49:15,16   Can a woman forget?
Isaiah 54:5   Thy Maker is thine husband
Isaiah 55:1   Come ye to the waters
Isaiah 55:6   Call upon the name of the Lord
Isaiah 55:6,7   Seek ye the Lord
Isaiah 57:15   High and lofty One
Isaiah 58:12   Raise up the foundations
Isaiah 60:1   Arise, shine, for thy light is come
Isaiah 60:19   Sun shall be no more thy light
Isaiah 63:9,10   Angel of His presence
Isaiah 66:22,23   And it shall come to pass
Jer 6:16   Stand ye in the ways
Jer 9:23,24   Let not the wise man glory
Jer 15:16   Thy words were found
Jer 17:14,15   Heal me, O Lord, and I shall be healed
Jer 24:7   I will give them a heart to know Me
Jer 29:13,14,11   Ye shall seek Me and find Me
Jer 33:3   Call upon Him and He will answer thee
Eze 20:11,12   I gave them My statutes
Eze 36:25,26   Ye shall be clean
Dan 3:25   Lo, I see four men
Hosea 6:3   Then shall we know
Joel 2:23   Be glad then, ye children of Zion
Micah 4:2   Come and let us go up
Zech 6:12,13   Behold the Man whose name
Zech 12:10   In that day there shall be a fountain
Zech 13:1   In that day there shall be a fountain
Malachi 3:16   Then they that feared the Lord
Matt 5:44,45   Love your enemies
Matt 6:26,28,29   Behold the fowls of the air
Matt 7:7   Call upon the name of the Lord

Matt 11:28,29 Come unto Him	Eph 1:3,4,6,7 Before the foundation
Matt 16:26 What is a man profited?	Eph 3:14-19 I bow my knees before the Father
Matt 17:5 This is my beloved Son	Eph 4:13 Till we all come in the unity
Matt 18:19,20 If two of you shall agree on earth	Phil 1:19-21 To live is Christ
Matt 19:14 Suffer little children	Phil 2:5 Let this mind dwell in you
Matt 25:5,6,10 Behold the bridegroom cometh	Phil 2:6,9 In the beginning was the Word
Matt 28:18-20 All power is given Him	Phil 2:12,13 Work our your own salvation
Matt 28:20 He will never leave you	Phil 3:13,14 This one thing I do
Luke 6:37,38 Judge not, and ye shall not be judged	Phil 4:6 Be careful for nothing
John 1:1 In the beginning was the Word	Phil 4:8 Think on these things
John 1:14 Word was made flesh	Col 1:26,27 Christ in you the hope of glory
John 3:16 For God so loved this little world	Col 3:4 When Christ who is our life
John 3:34,35 He whom God hath sent	Col 3:16 Let the word of Christ dwell in you
John 4:10,14 Living Waters	1Thess 4:16,17 Lord Himself shall descend
John 4:23 Hour cometh and now is	1Thess 5:16-18 Rejoice evermore
John 5:25,26 As the Father hath life in Himself	1Tim 2:5,6 There is one God and one mediator
John 5:39 Search the Scriptures	1Tim 5:21 I charge thee before God
John 6:27 Labor not for the meat	1Tim 6:15,16 Blessed and only Potentate
John 14:18,20 I will come to you	2Tim 1:7 God has not given us the spirit of fear
John 14:23 If a man love Me	2Tim 3:16,17 Search the Scriptures
John 17:3 And this is life	2Tim 4:8 Crown of righteousness
John 17:22,23 And the glory	Heb 7:25 He is able also to save them
Acts 1:11 Ye men of Galilee	Heb 8:1 We have such an high priest
Acts 2:38 Repent, repent, and be baptized	Heb 8:10 This is the covenant
Acts 4:12 Neither is there salvation	Heb 9:14 How much more shall the blood
Acts 24:14 This I confess unto thee	Heb 10:19,20 Boldness to enter
Rom 1:16 I am not ashamed of the gospel	Heb 10:23,24 Let us hold fast the profession
Rom 5:6-8,10 Saved By His Life	Heb 12:1,2 Looking unto Jesus
Rom 6:4 As Christ was raised up	Heb 13:5 He will never leave you
Rom 8:1,2 No Condemnation	James 1:2-5 Count it all Joy
Rom 8:9-11 If a man love Me	James 4:7,8 Submit yourselves therefore to God
Rom 8:32 He that spared not His own Son	1Peter 1:11 Prophecy came not in old time
Rom 11:33 O the depth of the riches	1Peter 1:3 I'm crucified with Christ
Rom 12:1,2 I beseech you therefore brethren	1Peter 3:15 Sanctify the Lord God in your hearts
1Cor 2:9 Eye has not seen nor ear heard	1Peter 5:6,7 Humble yourselves therefore
1Cor 5:7,8 Christ our Passover is sacrificed	2Peter 1:21 Prophecy came not in old time
1Cor 8:6 And this is life	1John 1:3 Truly our Fellowship
1Cor 10:1-4 Rock Was Christ	1John 1:9 If any man sin, we have a Comforter
2Cor 1:3,4 Blessed be God, even the Father	1John 2:1 If any man sin, we have an Advocate
2Cor 3:18 From glory to glory	1John 4:2 When Christ who is our life
2Cor 4:4,5 god of this world	1John 4:9 In this is manifested the love of God
2Cor 4:6 God who commanded the light	1John 4:18 No fear in love
2Cor 4:11 Word was made flesh	2John 3 And this is life/Grace be to you
2Cor 4:17 Our light affliction	3John 2 Beloved I wish above all things
2Cor 5:17 If any man be in Christ	Rev 3:12 Him that overcometh will I make
2Cor 13:5 He will never leave you	Rev 14:6,7,12 Fear God and give glory to Him
Gal 2:20 I'm crucified with Christ	Rev 15:3,4 Great and Marvellous are Thy Works
Gal 4:6 God has sent the Spirit of His Son	Rev 18:1 Arise shine for thy light is come
Gal 5:22,23 Fruit of the Spirit	

TEACH Services, Inc.
P U B L I S H I N G

We invite you to view the complete
selection of titles we publish at:
www.TEACHServices.com

We encourage you to write us
with your thoughts about this,
or any other book we publish at:
info@TEACHServices.com

TEACH Services' titles may be purchased in
bulk quantities for educational, fund-raising,
business, or promotional use.
bulksales@TEACHServices.com

Finally, if you are interested in seeing
your own book in print, please contact us at:
publishing@TEACHServices.com

We are happy to review your manuscript at no charge.

www.ingramcontent.com/pod-product-compliance
Lightning Source LLC
Chambersburg PA
CBHW082236170426
43196CB00041B/2812